ALSO AVAILABLE FROM PETER A. LAPORTA,

"IGNITE THE PASSION, A GUIDE TO
MOTIVATIONAL LEADERSHIP"

WWW.AUTHORHOUSE.COM

WHO HIRED THESE PEOPLE?

PETER A. LAPORTA

authorHOUSE®

AuthorHouse™
1663 Liberty Drive, Suite 200
Bloomington, IN 47403
www.authorhouse.com
Phone: 1-800-839-8640

First published by AuthorHouse 3/19/2009

ISBN: 978-1-4389-5699-2 (sc)

Library of Congress Control Number: 2009901959

Printed in the United States of America
Bloomington, Indiana

This book is printed on acid-free paper.

To book a speaker event, schedule a seminar, or inquire about

our consulting services, please access our website at

HTTP://LAPORTAENTERPRISES.COM

For Angel, who I fall in love with every
day of my life;

For Peter Jr., who taught me to be a father
all over again;

and

For the charmed ones, Amber, Hope, and
Sara, who each steal daddy's heart with
every breath they take.

TABLE OF CONTENTS

Forward

"Live like you were dying"

The day was January 8, 1985. It was a day that started out with the best of intentions and ended up changing my life forever. Just a few friends heading up to Okemo Mountain in Vermont for a great day of skiing. I remember driving up in Tom's Saab, with Doug and Steve trying to sleep in the back seat. I remember the day being extremely cold. I remember that the theme from The Andy Griffith Show was playing on the morning radio show that we were listening to and we all started whistling the tune as we approached the mountain. These are the minute details that set the tone for the day, but the rest of the morning remains fuzzy.

The temperature that day was no more than 50 degrees below zero at the top of the mountain with the wind chill factor. I know this for a fact because we all waited patiently for the temperature to rise to an acceptable level so that the lifts to the top would open for skiing. After hearing the announcement that the peak was opened, my friends and I immediately jumped on a chair lift to the top. Little did I know that this would be the last chair lift ride for me for several years.

The run from the top was very slick. Ice had formed on top of the fresh powder due to the temperatures and there was a crystal glaze on everything making it difficult to see anything. You could feel the snow crack and crunch as you maneuvered through the terrain. As we gained speed going over a crest, I felt a sudden vertigo as the snow beneath me gave way to the powder below. My body was thrust backward and sideways simultaneously and the impact was severe. Maybe it was the brittle cold, maybe just bad karma, but my right kidney was pushed against my rib cage with such force that it split in two. My initial reaction was that I had broken a rib. When I attempted to stand, I realized the situation was much worse as the world began to spin. The internal bleeding began to take affect immediately and things got very fuzzy, very fast.

I can't tell you the name of the rescue workers that got me down the mountain that day, but I can tell you that without their swift response I would not be here today writing about this story. I am eternally grateful to their skills and agility to get me to the base hospital. Upon arrival there, I was immediately worked on by a small team of nurses and emergency personnel. Although I do not know all the technical terms for the events that followed, I do know some key things happened.

When I first arrived at the base, the nurses could not find a pulse or a blood pressure reading. When they finally achieved a reading, it was 60 over zero. I was failing fast and needed attention. Unfortunately, my rapidly declining condition was beyond the realm of their emergency services and required a certified physician. Like a scene from the movies, an announcement went out on the mountain searching for a "doctor in the house". The angel that answered the calling was Doctor Jack Cassidy. He was skiing with his family and answered the call since he was near the base. Fortunately for me, he did not respond with, "I'm not working right now" or "it's not my department". He came to the base hospital and administered the miracle shot that got my heart and blood pumping again so that I was ready for the ambulance ride. Without Doctor Cassidy, the trip would not have been possible or necessary.

The ambulance ride from Okemo mountain to Springfield Hospital was difficult and life changing. I cannot tell you the technician's names that worked on me, nor the name of the driver, but what I can tell you is that I flat lined three times on the way to the hospital and each time I was brought back to life by their competent hands. The first flat line came and everything was a flash of white light. There was not much to remember from that first trip to the other side except waking up to the EMT pumping my chest and telling me to hang on and come back.

The second time my vitals flat lined I was thrown into an ascending cavern. Although I write this passage 23 years after it occurred, I could tell you every detail inside that cavern. The rippling walls giving way to a larger, smoother, more lit area at the top of the ascension. As I approached the upper lip to view the next area, I was pulled violently back to reality as the bells and alarms from the inside of the ambulance came back into focus. Once again, my life was saved by the skills of the EMT and the machines at his disposal.

My third trip to the other side when I flat lined does not need to be detailed here on this page. It is a personal story that I have never before shared except to my wife, but I am willing to talk about it to anyone who needs that much motivation in life. I can tell you that there is definitely an afterlife, definitely a judgment day and indisputably a greater God that controls it all. Once again my life was saved by total strangers, giving their all to yet another rider in their ambulance.

The rest of the story has many facets, some comical, some not. I won't take your time or test your patience by going through all the details. What I will tell you is that my life was touched by many more strangers that day, all doing the best possible job in a difficult situation. When I awoke for the first time in the critical care unit, there was a priest administering the last rights over me. Fortunate for me, I got the chance to interrupt him mid sentence before my fate could be sealed. All in all, it was not a good day to die.

I share this story with you for many reasons. First and foremost, it demonstrates the ultimate in customer service. The professionals in the healthcare industry take care of us every minute of the day and every patient takes it for granted in some shape or form. While we are complaining about the length of time associated with check in and processing so many forms, we forget that the information on these forms may save our life. All the information we give to these service providers allow them to better care for us while we are in their hands. We complain about the lines at the pharmacy windows, but we forget what would happen if the pharmacist were to rush and give out the wrong medication. We complain about the wait time in the doctors' office, yet relish every moment that he takes to care for you, the patient. For me, there is no greater customer service than that given by the healthcare industry. We trust them with our lives and the lives of our loved ones, allowing no room for poor customer service.

The second reason I share this story is that it drives home the point of second chances. When we are given another chance in life, it is for a reason. For me, I can only imagine that I was granted a second chance that day because there was so much more for me to do. To create new lives through my children and to touch thousands of lives along the way through my books, my leadership, and my seminars; maybe that was all part of the master plan. We are all given second chances in life, in love, and it is up to each one of us to seize the day. "Life is like a piano, what you get out of it depends on how you play it".

Since my last book reached people around the globe, my publisher has decided to give me a second chance to write again. Hopefully, in this book, you will not see the same mistakes I made last time. In fact, this book takes a different approach to the story telling I included in my last book, bringing aboard many encounters from all realms of the customer service world. Each story is followed up by an afterthought or a commentary on the events that transpired.

Restaurants, retail stores, banks, real estate, repair shops. Doctors, lawyers, mechanics, plumbers. The cable company, the phone company, the dreaded electric company. No matter what you do, no matter where you go, you will encounter some form of customer service in your day. From the first interaction to the last, every transaction has an opportunity to shape your day. If your first stop when you leave the house is the coffee shop and the lines are too long or the service is poor, it sets a negative tone to your day. If you start your vacation and the front desk clerk at the hotel is rude and lacks interpersonal skills, the rest of your stay will most likely be clouded.

Customer service is everything. It is the lifeblood of all business transactions. While most business owners will agree with that statement, they continue to lose sight of the big picture. They continue to recruit and hire poorly. They continue to rush their people through training and hope that in the end, they will get it. While individual actions dictate the outcome of customer service tragedies, it is important to remember that it is the responsibility of their leaders to act responsibly and put the right people in the right places. Have you ever noticed that you encounter the rudest people at the customer service desk?

Customer service and second chances walk a tight rope together. We never get a second chance to make a first impression. If the customer is patient we may or may not get a second chance to improve on customer service. Of the times we are granted a second audience, it is imperative that all the stops and whistles are pulled out.

In other words, "Live like you are dying". Embrace every moment you are granted on this earth. Since that cold day in '85, I have encountered many reminders to put my best foot forward. A motorcycle accident, three cancer scare operations, and numerous other close calls remind me daily to…

"Live as though today were my last, and work as if I will live forever".

PART ONE

THE LOSERS

1

IT'S JUST DONUTS AND COFFEE PEOPLE...

My wife and I have always been coffee drinkers. Not the kind of people you see walking around with mugs in their hand 24/7, but just people who appreciate a good cup of java. Unfortunately, our lives are so busy that we can never seem to make a pot of coffee and drink it. That requires time that we just don't have. In our hectic schedule, we are lucky to have time to drink a cup, let alone go through the whole creation process.

Be that as it may, we are constantly in search of coffee shops that can serve up a good cup of coffee in a fair amount of time, prepared the way we like it. Although this request sounds simple enough, if you are a coffee drinker you understand the dilemma. Some places offer good coffee, but you have to prepare it yourself and you pay through the nose for a cup. Other shops you stop at are a pot luck of surprises. What flavor do they have today? When was it made? Do they have cream, or just milk? You get the idea. Anyway, through all of our searches we happened upon the great Dunkin Donuts.

I can't tell you much about all of their product offerings, but I can tell you that their coffee is wonderful and the day they put in Drive up windows was the day they became my wife's hero. She can drive up to a microphone, tell someone how she wants her order, and within a minute or so, she has a perfect cup of coffee. Or so she thought. The practical application of this endeavor requires a minimal amount of customer service and the ability to listen to an order.

One bright sunny day, someone decided to build a Dunkin Donuts down the street from our house. When I say down the street, it can't be more than a mile down the road, or if you are desperately waiting for the caffeine to hit, around a minute to get there. My wife was thrilled. She could pick up a cup on her way to wherever she went. Going to work, get a cup. Going shopping, get a cup. Taking the kids to school, get a cup. Just too easy! And they even put in a drive thru! Unfortunately, when they put in the coffee makers and all of the other items needed to open the shop, they forgot to hire competent people.

My wife is a basic needs person. In her world, as well as mine, things come down to very basic requests. Her coffee is a prime example. In the world of coffee, she likes it prepared with a lot of cream and a little sugar. When the store first opened, she would ask for her coffee extra light, one sugar. Every day she would ask for the same coffee and get a multitude of variations. Finally, one day someone gave her a perfect cup of coffee. So perfect, in fact, that she circled around the building after trying it and returned to the line to talk to the person that prepared it.

When she finally came up to the window, the woman asked, "Is there anything wrong with your coffee."

My wife grinning from ear to ear simply replied, "No, it is perfect. I just wanted to find out how you made it so I can ask the other people that work here to make it exactly that way every time."

The woman laughed as though it were a big secret and explained that it had eight pumps of cream (from their dispenser) and one sugar. Perfect! She now had a formula for the perfect cup.

That afternoon, craving more of that perfect cup, she returned to the same Dunkin Donuts, but the woman had left for the day. So, thinking it was a simple request, my wife ordered a medium coffee with eight pumps of cream and one sugar. The person at the other end of the speaker asked her to repeat the order because they did not hear her correctly. My wife repeated her request and proceeded to the window. When she paid for her coffee and pulled away, she took a sip of her coffee and almost drove off the road gagging. The person seemed to have made the coffee with eight sugars and one cream!! Well, she chalked up the situation to a misunderstanding and continued on because she was on her way to an appointment.

The next day, she returned to the drive thru and asked for the same request. Medium coffee with eight pumps of cream and one sugar. Before pulling away she asked the person at the window how they made her coffee and they repeated back her order perfectly. Great, no problem. Except when she got on the highway and tried her coffee, it had eight creams and eight sugars. Again, no coffee. This ridiculous ritual went on for days. She finally found the woman who made her coffee perfect the one day and asked her where she had been. She explained she only works there part time and that she could only be there one or two days a week. My wife, thoroughly disappointed, asked the woman to talk to her fellow employees and explain to them how she wanted her coffee.

From that day and every day there after, my wife returned to that drive thru. Time after time her coffee was made wrong. She went inside and talked to the manager one day, who apologized and gave her a free cup of coffee. Of course, the coffee was made wrong again!

Since then, she has talked to the franchise owner and the corporate office, who all made excuses and offered free coupons and the like. The only bright idea someone had was to try a different location. Well, she did! And every other location in the Dunkin Donuts Dynasty has been able to follow those simple instructions and make a perfect cup for her.

Regardless of what state we travel to, if she finds a Dunkin Donuts she stops and puts in her request. Just about every time, it comes out perfect. A thousand miles away the coffee is perfect, but the coffee down the street from our house is never correct. What's the difference? The people. People who can't listen or won't. People who can't or won't follow a simple request from a customer. And yet, they keep their jobs in a customer service industry.

Who Hired These People?

Afterthought

"Excellence is the result of caring more than others think is wise, risking more than others think is safe, dreaming more than others think is practical, and expecting more than others think is possible"

Communication is a circular process. You may initiate a conversation by looking at another individual and stating your purpose. In return, that person listens to what you have said, thinks of a response, and replies back to you verbally or non- verbally. When you receive what they have replied back to you either visually or through audio recognition, you have completed the circle. No matter how many people you involve in the communication process, these key elements must be there. A message is sent and one is received. Simple enough.

In the realm of customer service, communication is not only a simple process, but the basis upon which customer service can exist. A customer sends a signal verbally or non- verbally, and then someone responds. How well the message is received is half of the problem. There must be clear, concise messages sent in a fashion that can be responded to in a correct fashion.

Have you ever called 411 on your telephone to seek out a phone number? The first thing that happens is a live person or recording asking "What city and state please?" You respond with your information.

"Orlando, Florida"

The system then responds correctly or incorrectly.

"You said Bando, Florida, correct?"

"No, Orlando, Florida!"

"O.K. Landeau, Florida, correct?"

"NO, O-r-l-a-n-d-o, Florida!!"

"O.K., I'm sorry, Orlando, Florida, what listing please?"

"LaPorta Enterprises"

"Porto Landscaping"

"No, LaPorta Enterprises"

"Is that with two G's"

"No G's, L-a-P-o-r-t-a Enterprises"

"O.K. Here it is. That number is…"

If it takes you ten minutes to get a number from information, should you still have to pay for it? After all, it caused you more grief than it would of if you looked it up yourself in a phone book. Maybe that is the motive behind all of the phone systems that have replaced human beings in customer service. The companies can reduce the number of service calls if they frustrate the people enough not to call. Maybe they know that you will never find the right choice when they put you into their phone que? Maybe they don't want you to be able to talk to an operator because that would cost additional labor funding and the number of actual complaints would increase exponentially. Makes you wonder!

If listening is half of the equation in communication and customer service, why are people in such a hurry not to listen to you? It is much like the frustration you get when you pull into a drive thru at a restaurant. As soon as you pull up to the menu board to make your choice, the person on the mike asks, "Can I take your order please?" If you respond that you need a minute or one moment please, you are pushing the envelope. Guaranteed, within 10-15 seconds the person will respond with, "Ok, are you ready". Hopefully, you were able to speed read the menu, the specials, the prices, and formulated your answer in proper form in that short time. If you have others in the car that also need to decide, forget it. The order taker will zone out after the first few words.

Wherever you go, whatever request you may have for service, listening becomes the key. The more precise your need for the service, the better the listening needs to be. If I order a cheeseburger with no ketchup, an order of fries with ketchup on the side, and a small juice for one of my kids, I know that order has to be right. If you don't repeat it back to me, I will repeat it for you. If not correct, my kids will cry, I'll get frustrated, and you will have to cook me new food.

On the other end of the spectrum, if my wife orders one thousand polo shirts for one of my seminars, the graphics need to be precise. There is no room for misspelled words or the delivery going to the wrong hotel on the wrong date (all of which have happened, by the way). When the person takes the order, they need attention to detail with approved graphics, lettering and precise instructions. If the business fails to listen to the details, there is a great chance that the order will be ruined and the customer will be dissatisfied.

Proper listening techniques therefore become the cornerstone of the customer service industry. If you are the one listening, it is up to you to create whatever process you need to understand the customer. Let's take a moment to review some of those techniques.

- *Do you have the proper tools required to listen to the customer?*

- *Do you have a pen and paper to write down the order?*

- *Is the phone or speaker system working properly so that you can understand what is being said by the customer?*

- *Is the customer service representative bilingual or do they have the resources to listen to customers in other languages?*

- *Do online order systems have user support with operators standing by?*

- *Does the customer service representative possess the patience and tolerance to take care of customers with a speech impediment or strong cultural accents?*

- *Is there ample time allotted for the customer to give their request and the service to be reciprocated?*

- *Is there software offered/utilized for repeat customers to streamline their request?*

All of the items listed are an excellent source to begin your improvement process. If you are a service provider, it is your responsibility to put forth your best effort to listen to whatever the customer has to say. Any shortcut that would circumvent these efforts would simply minimize the service you are giving to customers.

If and when you are on the customer side of the communication process, it is possible for you to make the transactions smoother.

- *First, know what you want. If you are not ready to make a decision yet, let them know. It is ok to be on an information gathering mission. If you are prepared with your decision, have your choices ready to convey to the person taking your order.*

- *Second, speak as clearly as you can. Understand that outside factors are at play here. There are the noises behind you, on the phone line, and background noise on the receiving end of things. If you are at the bank or any other drive thru service lane, understand that the noise of the car and those around you are interfering with your requests.*

- *Third, don't be afraid to ask clarifying questions to ensure your requests are clear. Did you get the right specifications on the window measurements? The linen I wanted was the sky blue not the royal blue.*

- *Fourth, ask for a printed copy of your request or simply have your order repeated back to you. You will be amazed at how many mistakes you will catch in this fashion. Better to catch the communication mistakes now before they become a larger issue once your service has been delivered.*

- *Finally, patience is a virtue and it will go a long way. If you are lucky enough to talk to a human being and not a phone machine or a computer monitor, the company is putting their best foot forward. But with that, they are giving you a human being that has their own set of attitudes, accents, and difficulties understanding. The patience that you take in the beginning will go a long way to completing your customer service request.*

Whether you are the customer or the person giving customer service, remember that listening is the key. If the communication breaks down, your request breaks down. Imagine what the world would be like if you didn't have to send back a steak because they cooked it the wrong way; if you didn't have to scramble on your wedding day because everything happened as you requested; if someone could actually count out eight creams and one sugar in a cup of coffee?

2

BANK OF WHAT COUNTRY???

After my first book was published, I started receiving many requests to talk to different groups about the subject matter. From just a few speaking engagements came a whole new business endeavor for me. I started traveling the world talking to businesses, organizations and schools about leadership and customer service. As you may have guessed, I am usually paid for these appearances from a variety of banking institutions around the globe. When I receive payment in check form, I generally deposit the money in my company account and wait for funds to clear.

At one point, I did a series of seminars for a company that had locations scattered across the country. Every time, the company would pay me by checks drawn on the Bank of America. Being a very large bank, their checks are easily identified and have never been a problem to process.

In August and September of 2004, the state of Florida was hit with an unprecedented four hurricanes in a row. The state was crippled. There was a loss of power throughout most of the state, creating chaos in everyone's lives. Even when power was restored, most businesses were kept closed for many days, some weeks. There were shortages of food, water, gas, and definitely money. Most ATM machines were shut down and businesses lost the capability to process credit or debit cards. Luckily, I had a check drawn on Bank of America.

Although nervous for not having cash around the house, I felt like I had the golden ticket because I had a check that I could cash. Luckily, my bank was open. I chanced the gas situation and drove over to the bank, which had served me well for many years. As I signed the check and passed it over to the clerk, I saw in her eyes that a downfall was coming. Since the bank had just reopened, many global systems were offline and there was no relief in site. She could not therefore, cash the check. The best she could do was to deposit the check into my account and wait for it to clear. She then suggested that I take it over to Bank of America where it was drawn. It was right down the road a few miles and she would call to verify they were operating correctly. Sure, just another five miles with no gas stations open, why would I get nervous?

As I pulled up to the Bank of America, I was slightly relieved to see a few cars being taken care of in the drive thru. The bank lobby was not open for another half hour, but this would work fine. As I drove into one of the lanes, I noticed a sign that indicated the following;

"Our drive thru is open from 8am to 9am daily for customers only"

Customers only? If you are doing business with the bank, you are a customer, correct? If you do business with any entity in the free enterprise system, you are the customer, aren't you?

Even if the sign referred to customers with direct business with the bank, I was covered. After all, the check was from a Bank of America account.

Right? Wrong!

As I approached the drive thru dispenser and inserted my check with verification, I sat back in relief.

After a few moments, a voice came through the speaker.

"Mr. LaPorta, do you have an account with this bank?"

"No, ma'am. But the check is drawn on an account from your bank."

"I'm sorry, sir, but the drive thru lane is for our customers only. You will have to come in the lobby once it opens."

"Excuse me? Why can't you cash the check that is drawn on your bank?"

"We can cash your check. Just not right now. You will have to come inside once the lobby opens."

"And your name is..? I just want to get it right when I talk to your manager."

"My name is Helen, and please clear the lane for one of OUR customers."

I drove away flabbergasted. How could this happen in my town? In my country? Is this not a form of discrimination? *We will only serve those people who are in this group.* What a crock!!!

Half an hour later, as I paced impatiently outside the bank, the lobby doors were opened. As I approached the window, a woman greeted me with the standard line, "May I help you?".

As the words began to form on my mouth, I looked down at here name tag. Of course it read, Helen.

"Sure Helen, maybe you could tell me why I just waited a half hour to speak to the same teller, with the same money in her drawer, about the same check drawn on this same bank."

"I told you sir, if you have a problem with the policy, you can speak to the manager."

"Sure, I'd love to. But first, let's cash this check. Here it is and here are my ID's."

After a few minutes of contemplation, Helen returned with the icing on the cake.

"Just to inform you, there will be a $5 fee for this transaction."

"What? Why would there be fee for cashing your own check? I don't charge myself a toll when I take money from one pocket and put it in the other, why would you charge a fee to cash your own check?"

"Do you want to pay the fee or not? I've had enough of your questions."

"Cash the check."

As I gathered up the bills and walked away from the counter, I was greeted by the bank manager.

"Can I help you sir"

"Well, ma'am. You could have helped me a half hour ago, but chose not to. Your bank could have helped me a minute ago by not charging ridiculous fees, but chose not to. And your teller, Helen, could have been pleasant, but chose not to."

"Then I suggest YOU choose to do business somewhere else!!"

As my jaw dropped to the ground, I restrained myself from retort and exited the bank from customer hell.

Rude bank + Rude policies= rude employees.
Go figure!!

Who Hired These People?

Afterthought

"The Character of any team is reflected in the standards it sets for itself"

There are hundreds of quotes that come to mind when I look back at this story. "The customer is always right". What happened to that basic premise in customer service? "Take care of the customer or someone else will". Apparently, if you have a very large scale operation that spans across the country, you don't have to worry about offending a few customers along the way. "The customer is not here for us, we are here for the customer". Well, you get the picture.

When conducting my seminars, dolling out consulting advice, or simply greeting anyone along the way, I consider every person I meet to be a customer. There are sub categories called, potential customers, book purchasers, current or past clients and a dozen other labels. But, no matter what file they happen to fall under, every person I meet in the self employed regime is a customer to me. I try to treat everyone with the utmost respect and patience and always look for something to learn from every encounter.

In the world of big business, rules seem to change. Companies take offensive stands and chalk them up under an umbrella called calculated risk. Rules don't necessarily get broken as much as they are bent. If we change this policy, we offend this many people potentially. If we administer this fee, only this many people will have a problem with it. How many times in business are we told that rules or fees are flexible? "Well, my boss says I have to charge this fee but since you are so nice, we'll just forget about it".

The question you have to ask yourself as either a consumer or a service provider is, *"Where does it end?"* There are numerous commercials out there that are hysterically funny in the answer to that question. To the case in hand, let's look at a competitive bank's commercial in the handling of bank fees.

"Hi, I just got my bank statement in the mail, can you explain it to me?"

"I can, but there is a bank statement explanation fee that I will have to charge on top of the fee for answering the phone"

"I'm sorry; did you say there was a fee for answering the phone?"

"Yes, in addition to the fee for the statement, there was an initial fee for answering the customer service hotline, and for every question you ask during the call?"

"Every question?"

"Yes, and that's another fee right there!"

This type of Abbott and Costello routine goes on and on as the rival bank pokes fun at its competitors.

"As far as your account is concerned, there is the monthly standard bank fee, the daily and weekly money holding fee, the standard ATM fees, the…"

"Wait, I didn't use any ATMs!"

"Yes, but someone has to pay for the ATMs to be there when you do need them"

"But.."

"Then we have this fee and that fee and another fee, and another, and another…"

ENOUGH IS ENOUGH!!

*Although this commercial and many like it stress the ridiculous fees that are imposed by banks, they are definitely not alone. Have you looked at your home or cell phone bill lately? I am constantly amused by ads that state that you can have a phone for only (x) amount per month. What they really are stating is that the **base** fee is (x) amount. On top of that, you will be billed for this tax and that tax, this fee and that fee. All of a sudden your great deal of $30 per month is actually a $100 bill in your mailbox each month.*

As a consumer, a husband, and a father of four, I always question the fees. Every person should! I have found that in most cases, the fees cannot be explained with a great degree of credibility. Ask a time share salesman to justify maintenance fees. That question went unanswered for so many years that the industry has begun changing the name of the fees to confuse the consumer. Why are you getting hook up fees on your cable bill that you have had for three years running? Do they come out and unhook you every month just to charge you a new hook up fee?

When you are having carpet installed, why is there a delivery fee and an installation fee on the same bill? Don't the installers need to bring the carpet with them if they are going to install it? What about the plumbers and electricians that charge you a house call fee when they come to repair your pipes? If their job is to fix your leaking pipes, why would you pay an additional fee for the house call? It's not as if you can bring the pipes to their office. Your house is their office!!

What about auto repair! Why the diagnostic fee if they repair the vehicle? Didn't they have to find out what was wrong before they fixed it? Imagine if doctors worked the same way. First, you would have the waiting room fee. Then the nurses escort fee. The doctors five minute look at you fee. The diagnosis fee which would definitely be followed up with the prescription and instructions upon release fees. Sound ridiculous? Of course it is! But we allow auto repair shops to do the same thing with every repair. If you look at the final invoice, you will be shocked to see a breakdown of ridiculous fees that include but are not limited to diagnostic fees, vehicle storage (you know, for the three days it took them to fix your car), auto parts, auto core charge (which they get back when they bring them your old part), part disposal (their garbage fee), and much, much, more.

These are just a sampling of some of the fees that are charged to you, the consumer, on a regular basis. My purpose in highlighting them is simply to bring your attention to a world of customer service that is often overlooked. The going trend is to give you more service or continue old service at a price. It has become a magician's world of smoke and mirrors in an attempt to make you feel like you are getting more without the feeling that you were taken.

If you are a business or a service provider, read the writing on the wall! Don't nickel and dime us any more! We want full service without all the B.S.! If my bill is going to be $100 every month, let me know that up front so that I can figure it into my budget. Don't hide the fees in a complex disclosure statement that consumers cannot decipher nor understand. Put meaning and purpose behind the fees that you must charge us. If you are cashing your own check that was drafted by your institution and is staying at your institution, there is no logical answer on the face of the planet to charge the customer a fee.

Finally, remember the basic principles of customer service. You are here to serve the customer. You need us, the consumers, more than we need you. There will always be another bank, another mechanic, another real estate agent right down the road. Before you slap on some exorbitant closing cost on the sale of a house just because you can, remember that the guy down the street will fill out the same paperwork for the same house at half the cost. It is a market of free trade and free choice. Sooner or later, the customer will figure out that the bank next door gives free money orders and you don't have to be a bank "customer" to get one!

3

DINER DAYS AND DINER NIGHTS

Consistency is the cornerstone of customer service. As consumers, we respond to companies based on their ability or inability to provide customer service on a consistent basis. If an establishment treats you poorly every time you enter their doors, you eventually stop going there. On the other hand, if you are treated like a king and admonished each time you walk through the doors, you will be a customer for life. Unfortunately, most places fall somewhere between these extremes and we continually place a question mark next to their name.

When I was a teen growing up in the small New England town of Monroe, Connecticut, life was pretty basic. Every weekend, you would try to get a date, and if not, hang out with your friends at one of a few local haunts. Depending on which way the quiet excitement took you, by the end of the night there was always a trip to one of two diners.

If you have not experienced a true diner experience in New England, you have definitely missed out on a piece of Americana. The difference between these diners and others across the states is in their presentation. New England Diners are a big deal and in many towns, they represent the largest restaurants around. The layout inside their doors vary, but usually include a very small bar area, a large dining room with a choice of booths and tables, and a half dozen stools or so at a counter. In New England diners, you almost always encounter some posh display of desserts and sweets in some kind of outlandish display case near the front door. The menus inside are generally extensive and explore a wide variety of tempting dishes, from a simple sandwich or egg platter to prime rib dinners or stuffed lobster. As you can probably guess, I have spent more than my share of time inside these diner doors.

One of my favorite diners in the world is the Blue Colony Diner located in the beautiful town of Newtown, Connecticut. When I lived in that area, it was just minutes from my house and a great place to stop on the way home from a night out. In diner world, the Blue Colony Diner lives up to every classic expectation of the formidable experience. The approach to the diner heightens your senses as you get off the scenic Route 84 to a picturesque wooded area. As you enter the doors, you are greeted by a gentleman host and directed towards one of many locations. As you walk past the dessert display cases, your mouth waters at the pleasures you see before you. Pies, cakes, puddings, giant oversized cookies and Italian pastries fill your senses with delight as the host brings you to your dining destination.

After you are seated, you are presented with a very large menu with plenty of items to choose from. No matter what time of day (open 24 hours), or what day of the week, these basic elements are the same for every customer. Great location, beautiful restaurant, excellent menu. What more could you ask for?

Recently, I was giving a keynote speaker address in New York City, and had set aside a day to hop over to western Connecticut to visit some friends and relatives. On the way into the state around mid-day, my wife and I decided to stop off for another amazing meal at the Blue Colony Diner.

From the moment we entered the front doors, we were not disappointed. The bakery items jumped out at us and we made a note to pick some up on the way out to bring to our relatives. Once seated, a friendly smiling server came to our table and greeted not only my wife and I, but the children as well. Before being asked, she brought over crayons and coloring papers to keep the children occupied during their visit. She informed us of the daily lunch specials and took our beverage orders.

Within minutes, she returned with our drinks, with special cups and covers for the kids to prevent any accidents from happening. After taking the orders for my wife and I, she suggested many alternatives for our two little ones and our sometimes finicky teenage daughters. We followed her suggestions and were pleasantly pleased with the results.

The food was excellent, perfectly portioned and we didn't have to spend a bankroll to please the kids. What more could a parent ask for. As we were leaving, she gave the two youngest ones a little pinch on the cheek and told them to come visit her again soon. Without being planned, we would soon find out when we would revisit.

Although time was short, we had promised both my wife's family and mine a visit that afternoon. Since the first stop took longer than expected, we suggested to my relatives to meet them for dinner on our way back to the city. They suggested the Blue Colony since time was short, and we agreed. Even though we had eaten there for lunch, their menu had plenty more to offer us for a different meal. Besides, the customer service had been excellent earlier that day.

As our second meal in the same day began, we became very aware that it is the people that make all the difference in customer service. We were seated at a table with our guests by the host who stated that the server would be over shortly. Although we requested the wonderful woman from earlier in the day, she had left already. The server who would take care of our table was entirely different.

After waiting ten minutes for her to approach the table, our server came over and simply asked, "Are you ready to order". No greeting, no explanation of dinner specials, no congeniality. After taking our drink orders, we stopped her from running away quickly by asking for a second high chair for one of the children who would not sit still in her seat. The reply we received was totally unexpected.

"You should have asked the host for the high chair. Now I have to go find one"

With that, she left the table to return ten minutes later with our drinks and no high chair. Again we asked for the seat and were told she will look again, but she was busy. We were able to flag down the host who was more than happy to get us a second high chair.

He had the same cordial smile as he did when we were here for lunch, even though his day was getting to be quite long.

When the server finally returned to our table to take our dinner orders, we informed her that time was getting tight as we had an appointment in the city to get to. The only response we received was that it was a busy night. (so, basically deal with it!)

The meal, or lack of it, seemed to progress at the same snail speed. The salads came ten or fifteen minutes later as my two younger children seemed to rev up to their highest irritability. In an attempt to soothe the screams, my wife asked the server if we could get the children's food first and begin feeding them. She shrugged her shoulders and walked away, stating "We'll see". After another block of time had passed, she arrived with everyone's food, EXCEPT the children's. She said it would take them another moment or two. The icing on the cake was only a moment away as the server quickly planned her retreat. As she placed the last dinner plate on the table, she pulled her hands back quickly and accidentally turned a bowl of gravy over onto my baby's lap.

As parents of four children, we fully understand that accidents will happen. We are fully seasoned in the art of forgiveness and tolerance, since many such moments have occurred over the years. However, one thing we can never tolerate is the lack of compassion once a mistake has been made.

"Oh, want some extra napkins?"

Those were the words that came from the server's mouth.

There were no apologies. No care for the baby. Just the phrase, "oh, want some extra napkins?"

The moments that followed can be pieced together on your own. Tempers flared, patience found its way out the door, and the rest of the evening was a wash. Since we were late already, there was no time to sit and argue. The management team from the restaurant handled the situation very delicately and professionally. Ultimately, they saved a life long customer from never returning to their restaurant. The kids never got to eat there and settled for a quick bite while sitting in Manhattan traffic.

Day shift, night shift, or third shift.

Weekday or weekend.

Same restaurant. Why the difference? Why the complete turn around in customer service?

(Author's note: We still frequent this wonderful diner every time we are in that part of the country. However, the owner has eliminated some of the inconsistencies listed above to ensure a great dining experience every time)

Who Hired These People?

Afterthought

"*Great customer service does not just happen by circumstance. It is a determined effort to carry through every moment of every day*"

Consistency is the life blood of any business. If you make a great pizza today at noon, you should make a great pizza everyday. There should not be any excuses for varying temperatures affecting your dough, varying distributors affecting your sauce, and definitely no differences in the hands of the pizza maker.

Although well versed in business doctrines, I am constantly amazed at restaurants, retailers, and so many others using a time of the day or day of the week to highlight great customer service.

"Early bird special, two for the price of one if you order dinner at 3pm"

"Kids eat free, with each purchase of an adult entrée every other Tuesday after 5pm"

"Now Serving Prime Rib, available only on Monday and Tuesday nights after 6pm"

"Holiday special: shop between 4am and 6am and receive free wrapping paper"

You know the gimmicks. You've heard them all. If you were to ask the retailers or restaurant owners the reasoning behind these specials, they would most certainly bring up customer service for one of their reasons. At this point, you have to ask how and why. How is serving people their dinner at 3pm going to be beneficial to the customer? Why would anyone want to eat that early? The only benefit here is to the business that gets to fill some empty seats during a down time in the day. As far as kids meals that are free, why not every day? Why all the stipulations? If you want to provide some extra service to the parents while driving your profits, let them control what night of the week they can treat the kids.

As a retail manager for the greater portion of my adult life, I can honestly say that the early bird shopping experience is one of the most detrimental customer service experiences a retailer can offer. The retailer offers what are called "price leaders" to entice the customer to their store early in the day while their pockets are full and their credit cards are not. However, in their guise to offer excellent bargains, most retailers break every rule in the book getting there.

First and foremost, they create ridiculous shopping hours. They force their workers who normally get a full night's sleep, to get to work in the middle of the night. Bleary eyed, still bloated from the turkey they ate for dinner the night before, they take a stand at their registers and prepare for the worst. As the doors are opened, customers with the same physical ailments are crushed and pushed as if the gates were opening on the great land rush. The stampede has begun and there is no room for the weak or timid. The customers are unhappy to be there in the middle of the night, almost as much as the workers who are forced to be there. The only thing that might save them is to actually find the deal they came here for.

The second huge disservice now comes to the customer. Although laws differ from state to state, there is always some degree of deception that occurs with these sales. If the big box retailers can offer a big screen television for only $50, you know that there will be only a few of them available. Every year, we look at the news at the end of these Black Fridays and are amazed that people get into fist fights or worst because retailers have created this nightmare.

When my wife and I set out to shop for the holidays, we always try to avoid such gimmicks. The stores that we give our dollars to earn that right by consistently having good prices and great customer service. Sure, we might save a buck here or a few pennies there by battling other human beings, but we save a little more holiday spirit by doing it our way.

If you take the same retailers that offer these sales and ask them if they would want this to happen every day, I'm sure the answer would be profound. One has to draw the question then as to why the inconsistency? Why offer something one day that you cannot offer the next. Specials come and go but the basic service should be there day or night, week day or weed end.

The best example of this inconsistency in customer service just to increase revenue has to be Denny's Restaurants. (They originally had their own chapter in poor service, but they fit in so well here). For those unaware, Denny's is a chain of full service restaurants that are very similar to the diner experience mentioned at the beginning of this chapter. In fact, many restaurants in their chain have changed their name to Denny's Diner in honor of the experience.

Among their many claims in customer service, the best substantiated one is that they are always open. As a twenty-four hour restaurant, Denny's offers you breakfast at any hour. Eggs at three in the morning are great if you are in the mood. However, at what cost? Are you willing to pay double for those eggs at that hour? How about triple? If you think that my exaggerating has hit a new high, you only have to frequent a Denny's late night.

At the bewitching hour of 10pm nightly, Denny's rolls out their late night menu. Across the board, their menu items become escalated in price. If you work second or third shift and have to dine at these late hours nightly, you better bring along more money for the experience. A typical breakfast that might be $2.99 or $3.99 during the morning hours is now available to you for $5.99 or $6.99. The same egg sandwich you get in the morning is double the price during the late night.

As if the higher prices weren't enough to drive you away as a customer, Denny's also limits their menu during these hours. If you are craving something healthier late night, then maybe you should not stop here. Salads aren't on the menu although the lettuce is still in the cooler. There are no prepared vegetables as side dishes to oppose the fried options. Want a baked or mashed potato as an option to their fried equivalent, no such luck.

Being the frequent inquisitor, I often ask the Denny's managers to justify the higher prices and limited offerings. In response, I am told that it is more expensive to operate a restaurant around the clock. They have to pay their late night workers higher salaries, so why not pass the costs onto the customers? They certainly can't be expected to offer the same menu items at all hours, it's just not feasible!

Feasibility must therefore fall into the eye of the beholder. I'm not sure what my reaction would be if I pulled into an all night gas station and found out that they only offer one grade of gasoline during late hours and that the price of it was higher per gallon than it is during the day. If the gas station attendant told me it just wasn't feasible any other way I might just have a heart attack right then and there.

Bottom line here is that customers should be offered the same products and the same great service every hour of every day. If you smile broadly for the first customers of the day, the last customers should receive the same welcome. If you offer an automated system for customer service, it should be available around the clock, not just during "normal business hours", whatever that means these days. We live in a global marketplace, and although not all businesses are available to customers twenty four hours a day, they need to be aware that customers may want their products and services at alternative hours.

From the first customer to the last and every phone call in between, the reputation of your business is on the line with every customer. If you believe in putting your best foot forward, don't ever show your bad foot. Cleanliness, safety, speed of service, pricing, and general customer service should be consistent every moment of the day. If you have an employee that doesn't adhere to this ideology, correct their actions or replace them. Consistency will always be the life blood of any business!

4

DMV

Three letters that bring out the very worst in every human being that operates a motor vehicle. Most people would rather have multiple root canals than to sit in the motor vehicle lines for hours. Before going into this story, I should probably say that that many states go out of their way to give extra customer service in the DMV offices. Florida, for example, separates the registration/tag offices from the license bureaus, to minimize lines. Many states have brought in television monitors, piped in music, and even allowed snack bars to open to make your wait more pleasurable. But in their quest to lift up levels of customer service, some have forgotten the simple things.

Like most Americans, I have a private vault of stories all about the DMV. We could talk about traffic violations, lines, forms, and the rude people but this story stands out as being unique. In order to handle the volume of business in the northeast markets, we opened a second office for LaPorta Enterprises in Connecticut. I relocated my family from Florida to Connecticut for a short time and was forced to get my drivers license transferred. As I attempted to find a parking space in the mayhem of a parking lot, I knew that the day would be long and the lines longer, but I sucked it up and entered the facility.

The building was set up like a series of cattle lanes. You went to one line for your forms, a second to process paperwork, a third to pay for your license, a fourth to take your picture, and a fifth to pick up the finished product. Each line was a perfect depiction of human emotion.

The people in the first line were reasonably optimistic and a few folks actually had signs of a smile in the corners of their mouth.

If you dared to look down to the other lines, you saw people sweating, looking at their watches, aggravation splattered all over their faces. The faces at the end could almost be labeled maniacal. It's no wonder that driver's license pictures in this state were all of miserable people!! The photos are taken after being in three or four other lines, for an untold number of hours!

After a brief stop in the information line to get direction, I proceeded on to the forms line to start the process. The internal clock started to tick off as I watched each patron approach the counter to get their forms. I inched along and after about twenty minutes, I received my forms and was directed to fill them out and take my place in the next line. Along the walls of the building were tall desk tops to fill out your paperwork, much like you would find in the post office. As I approached one of these countertops, it struck me odd that the desks had no pens on them. There was no place for a pen or even one on a chain. How bizarre!! No pens to fill out the forms; forms that you could not get until you arrived at the DMV!

In college, I had a roommate named Tom who taught me one of the best lessons I learned at UCONN. Never, ever, leave the house without a pen in your pocket! No matter where you go, no matter what you do, someone somewhere will need to use the pen. That lesson has never failed me, and I have Tom to thank for it. If this is not one of your normal practices, try it for a day. At the end of the day see how many times the pen has been used or asked to be used and you will be amazed.(Just don't forget to get it back so you still have it at the end of the day!)

Anyway, I was able to fill out my forms with no problem because of my trusted ball point pen. As I filled out the papers in triplicate, I noticed a young woman juggling two young children getting quite irate because she couldn't find a pen.

"I can't believe they expect me to fill out theses stupid forms and they refused to give me a pen to fill them out. 'Take a step over there and fill out these forms'. With what, I asked them. Shall I use my kids crayon? This is ridiculous!!"

Being the consummate gentleman, I offered the woman my pen to use.

"Thank you, but that's not the point. She told me I could buy a pen from the vending machine. Can you believe that, buy a pen to fill out their crummy forms! I told her I didn't have change and she just shrugged her shoulders, like she could care less."

"Ma'am, if you won't take my pen, maybe I could just buy you one, or give you the change for one, your choice".

"No, that will be the day that I give these idiots one more quarter than they deserve. I'll drag my kids home and fill out the forms and I'll be back another day. What a waste!"

As I looked out the door I watched the woman push her stroller with her kids out to the car. It was very obvious that a single writing instrument had completely destroyed her day. Her husband, her kids, and everyone she came into contact with would soon hear about her day at the pen-less DMV.

When I finally got up to the second of my clerical windows to process my license, I asked the woman who waited on me what was the situation with the pens. Was there a shortage of pens in Connecticut or was this just an oversight on the part of the DMV?

"No, we know there are no pens. We don't put them out for a reason. We used to give out pens and they never came back. We tried the chain thing and people would break the chain and steal the pen. So, to heck with it. Let them cough up a quarter and buy one for themselves. Not my problem."

Who Hired These People??

Afterthought

"Always give customers more than they expect to get"

The alternate quote selection for this afterthought was, "Your attitude in life will always determine your altitude in life". Either way, the lesson learned here is that the climate of a business is controllable. Through the years, the Department of Motor Vehicles has gotten a bad reputation. I'm not sure when it began or how, but I am sure that most Americans have the same preconceived notion that they will have a bad experience when they go to this business.

Because the threshold is so low, when the odd occurrence does happen and someone has a not so bad day at the DMV, they tell everyone they come into contact with.

"I had to get my license renewed today and, it went pretty fast, can you believe it? I was in and out of there in like twenty minutes! And look how good my license came out".

If you look at that person's picture, I would be fairly certain that they are smiling, still in control of their emotions and their time. The sad reflection on the other side of the coin is that most people will not bother complaining about their miserable trip to the DMV because the response they get is generally the same. "What did you expect?"

The Department of Motor Vehicles is one of the most infamous recipients of the bad customer service awards. As such, there is no motivation for them to change the world they exist in. Why bother going faster? People will still think they take their time. Why open more lanes or hire more personnel? People will continue to think there is not enough help there. Why bother to change?

With this defeatist attitude, stagnancy or lack of change is eminent. They have accepted their destiny and changed their attitude accordingly. The opinion will always be for bad service, so that is what they will give. Dentists, lawyers, and mechanics, all have similar negative viewpoints about their business, but many seek to overcome.

Here in Central Florida, more and more ads have popped up to change the viewpoints of the consumer towards theses businesses. You see billboards toting Dentist's message that they treat chickens (scared patients, that is).

"A trip to the Dentist does not have to be a painful experience"

"The lawyers that care"

'We don't get paid unless you win the case"

"The cleanest mechanic in town"

"No long waits for car repair"

"...lawyers, For the People"

All of these ads hope to reverse the stereotypes that customer service from a Dentist means pain, from a lawyer means money, and from a mechanic means a long wait. They refuse to accept what is expected and raise their service levels to surpass the customers' viewpoints. Does it work? Would your viewpoint on these classic professions change if you saw these ads or slogans?

Conversely, it is very possible for companies to have the opposite expectations thrown upon them. Take for example the Four Seasons hotel chain, or any other five-star resort. From the moment you inquire about a room at the Four Seasons, you expect a certain degree of customer service. That level is set very high depending on your prior experiences or simply by name recognition. Either way, the company has very high expectations from every customer that walks through their door. Accordingly, the Four Seasons hires, trains, and motivates their people to not simply meet, but exceed every customer's expectations.

Prior to your arrival at the hotel for your stay, their concierge contacts your people to inquire about the small details. Is there a daily paper that the guest reads? If so, the hotel will arrange for that paper to be delivered to your doorstep every morning. Is there a particular dietary preference or need that the chefs can prepare? If so, the concierge makes it happen. Their attention to customer service details makes them one of the best hoteliers in the world.

With such a reputation in tact, the hotel operates daily on a level unsurpassed in the industry. Accordingly, the price tag for a stay at one of their hotels is quite high. The few, the proud, the wealthy make this their playground as they circumnavigate the globe. They don't need to worry about what service they will receive because of their reputation.

However, every now and then, an incident occurs. Perhaps that incident is by no means the fault of the hotel but it influences their guests none the less. Let's say, for example, that a very prestigious guest is expecting a delivery to the hotel prior to their arrival. For discussion purposes, let's say that the delivery is monumental to closing a big business deal the next day.

The guest arrives at the hotel in customary fashion, has a flawless check in and retires to their suite to prepare for the next days battle. However, the materials they expected to find waiting in the suite are not there. The guest contacts the concierge desk and inquires about the delivery. The inevitable is confirmed that no package has arrived for the guest. Providing the highest level of service, the concierge offers to track down the package and guarantee the arrival.

As the hours pass into the evening, the guest becomes weary and aggravated. Soon enough, the problem becomes the hotel's problem.

"How could a hotel such as the Four Seasons lose my package?"

"Our apologies sir, but we never received your package."

"How can a hotel such as this not find my package?"

"Our apologies again, sir. I assure you we are doing everything possible to obtain your package."

The hours continue to pass and still no package. The time to reschedule the early morning meeting has come and gone. The guest is certain that a hotel with this reputation will come through for him in the end. However, as luck would have it, the package information is retrieved around midnight. The delivery was on the wrong transport plane and is now headed to the other side of the world. There is no chance that documents needed can be turned around in time for the early morning meeting. The guest is devastated.

As the realization of the pending disaster kicks in, the guest become irate and belligerent. The hotel, with all of its infinite resources should have had better control of the delivery. The hotel should have tracked the package from the moment it left his office. The whole business trip has been *ruined. The whole trip is a waste. The hotel is responsible for the loss of the business deal!*

As far fetched as this scenario is, situations like this occur around the globe in the hospitality industry. To assimilate the relevance, let us ponder the following question. What would the difference be if the same scenario happened at a Motel 6, a Best Western, or a Holiday Inn? Would the guest's expectations be as high? Would the guest have trusted the hotel to handle it in the first place if they knew they were just staying in a room at the Motel 6? Probably not. The guest would have held onto those documents through his whole travel itinerary, knowing that there is no way he could trust the hotel to take care of them.

If for some reason the package was still sent via some carrier, then the fault of the malfunction would fall directly on the carrier. The carrier should have had better control of the delivery. The carrier should have tracked the package from the moment it left his office. The whole trip is ruined. The whole trip is a waste. The carrier is responsible for the loss of the business deal.

The complete difference between the two lies in the expectations of the businesses involved. At the Four Seasons, the guest holds such high and almost unrealistic expectations of the hotel. At the Motel 6, the expectations are so low that the guest finds other people to blame for the mishap, or controls the whole situation themselves. Either way, a mistake was made and someone's day got ruined. It just depends on how you look at it.

The woman in the DMV story had a terrible day at the DMV. But was the day ruined simply because of a pen? The answer is no. Her day was ruined because she had to go to that miserable place, the DMV. No one has a good day at the DMV. No one has a good day at the dentist. No one has a good day when he or she has to talk to a lawyer. No day can be good if you have to take your car into the shop. Right? I guess not. Besides, isn't it always raining on those days anyway?

5

"Customer Service is Now Closed"

"Attention Wal-Mart shoppers, Customer Service is now closed".

That is the greeting that we received over the loud speaker as my wife and I entered the giant department store. Although the store was open twenty four hours a day, three hundred and sixty five days a year, the customer service department had apparently closed up shop. No more customer service today. That should have been the giant warning signal not to proceed any further, but we had a few items to pick up before going home that night.

With four children to take care of and a company to run that takes us all over the globe, quiet time together is often scarce. Sometimes, the big date for the week boils down to going shopping for a few things during some stolen moments in time. The rest of the evening would have to be in the comforts of our home as we unwind.

Our first stop was to pick up some candles for the evening. Unfortunately, the store was going through a remodel and everything had moved around since the last time we were there. Tracking down one of the many associates that were working, we had high hopes of a quick find on our treasure hunt.

"Excuse me, can you tell us where the candles would be?"

"Sure, that's an easy one; they are in the home furnishings area."

Laughing, my wife replied, "Ok, but the home furnishings department isn't there anymore, do you know where they moved it to?"

"You know, they moved that a couple days ago. I have no idea to where. Try asking the service desk."

With that reply, he scurried down the aisle and was gone. Back to the hunt, because of course, the service department was closed. As we continued our trek, we came across helpful service associate two.

"Excuse me, can you tell me where the candles moved to?"

"No English", kept walking.

This was turning into a rude festival. There was no attempt to navigate the English language. There was no attempt to mime what we were trying to locate with hand gestures. There was no attempt to locate an English speaking Wal-Mart associate. There was no attempt at customer service what so ever. She might have just told us to go fly a kite and we would have been greeted better. Nothing at all. Just a "No English" to tuck away in our insult file for the day.

With no faith in the associates that were left in the area, we just kept looking. Eventually, we tracked down the candles on the other side of the store. They were located next to the hardware department. Not sure what the logic was there, but we chalked it up as a temporary location and moved on to other shopping needs.

The next items on the list were located on the grocery side of the store. A little cheese and crackers, perhaps a bottle of wine, and we would be all set for a night of relaxation. Luckily the food side of the store had not changed too much so it was not too difficult to find the items that we wanted. The crackers were in the cracker aisle, the wine with the beer in the spirits section. No problem. As usual, we saved the best for last. The deli department.

If you have ever had the misfortune to walk up to the deli department at Wal-Mart, my sympathy goes out to you. No matter which store you choose in whatever town you come upon, the Wal-Mart deli department knows one speed, SLOW! It does not matter whether there are three people in line, or thirty, you should resolve yourself that a wait is on the horizon. This night was no exception. We talked about some alternative suggestions, but we were both set on some provolone cheese to complete the search. We picked a ticket and stepped aside.

As we waited for our number to come up, we looked at the few other people waiting and could not help but to chuckle. Each little waiting party was well prepared for their wait. One woman had brought along a magazine to read, another was looking at recipe cards. One man was holding a private meeting on his cell phone while another read the sports section from the daily paper. The scene resembled passengers waiting to board a plane, not a few consumers waiting for their favorite lunchmeat.

Time ticked on and our number was finally called. It was time to venture into the realm of deli service.

"*54*"

"Hi, we have number 54. Can we get a one pound chunk of provolone cheese, preferably off the end?"

"*Que?*"

"Do you speak any English?"

"Yes, little, you want Provolone?"

"Yes, please. A one pound chunk of provolone cheese. Off the end, if you can."

"You want thick slice?"

"I'm sorry," my wife pleaded, "You're just not understanding me."

"No, no, I understand". With that, the girl in the deli turned her back and went on her own little mission.

We watched with anticipation as she ventured into the deli case and pulled out the provolone cheese. O.K. Good sign. We watched even closer as she walked over to the slicing machine and put the cheese in its place. While operating in her own little world, the woman went about her business of slicing thick pieces of provolone cheese into the wax paper. The noise from the machine must have prevented her from hearing our interruptions from the other side of the counter. After slicing up a pound she turned and put the sliced cheese onto the scale.

"No, I'm sorry. You did not understand. I want one slice, one thick chunk of provolone cheese. Not for sandwiches, for cutting."

"Yes, I cut thick slice. One pound."

"No, you cut many slices, adding up to one pound. Not what I want."

The crowd behind us began to mumble. They were a mixed group with half of them laughing at the idiocy of the situation and the others frustrated at the growing line.

As if on cue, another Wal-Mart employee walked by at that moment and the deli girl called out for assistance. The girl approached the counter and the two of them had a quick conversation in Spanish. Without any explanation, the visiting clerk turned and walked away quickly. The girl behind the counter tossed the cheese aside, shrugged her shoulders and proceeded to call the next number.

My wife and I were in awe. What was going on? Where is the service? Where is our cheese? Where do we go, customer is service is closed, presumably forever. As we turned in amazement and started to walk away, we were greeted by the visiting clerk, a member of management, and a security guard. Apparently we were wrong. We were going to get service and get it fast.

"Is there a problem here?" The manager opened the conversation with a tone that was surprising to both my wife and I.

"Yes. We are just trying to get a one pound chunk of provolone cheese cut. We asked her if she could cut it off the end. Instead she cut up sliced cheese. I think it was just a misunderstanding with the language barrier."

"Why, don't you speak Spanish? You can't expect to live in Florida and not know Spanish."

In the flash of an instant, the manager was able to achieve an insult on our intelligence and apparently judge where we should live if we are not bilingual. With tempers starting to flair, I tried to diffuse the situation.

"Look, right or wrong, English or Spanish, we would just like our cheese so that we can leave. Is that too much to ask?"

"That's fine", the manager replied, "but I think you owe the girl an apology".

"An apology, for WHAT???"

"Well, you obviously insulted her, that's why she sent for me."

"We did nothing of a sort. My husband and I have been quite patient and understanding. We will not apologize for speaking English in America."

The manager turned abruptly and went behind the deli counter. With no sense of cleanliness or safety, he pulled out the tube of cheese and slammed it onto the counter. Grabbing a large knife, he cut off a chunk, threw it on wax paper and put it on the scale. Within moments he stuffed it in a bag, put the label on the package and handed it to my wife.

"Here's your cheese. I hope if you continue to shop at this store, you go out and learn some Spanish. It will make things a lot easier."

"Sure, we can make it a lot easier for you."

With that final remark, we turned, left our shopping cart, and walked out of the store, never to return to that Wal-Mart.

We finally realized that customer service at Wal-Mart had closed long before we got there and would probably never come around again.

Who Hired These People?

Afterthought

"Communication is a flowing river that knows no boundaries, that has no limits and has no end, as long as there are thoughts that need to be conveyed."

Communication. The spoken word. A gesture, a smile, an inflection. To special needs people it may be the positioning of your fingers or hands, or a combination of all of the above. Although I have been communicating with others since the moment of my birth, the vast universe of communication never hit home until my son was born.

Peter A. LaPorta Jr. was born almost four years ago at writing. He came to the world in the usual way, just like his three sisters before him. As he grew through his first year he communicated as any child would. He screamed when he was hungry, tired, or wet. If you are a seasoned parent, you learn which scream goes to which ailment. If you are a new parent, it may take you much longer to learn which form of communication your child is attempting.

As he crested his first year, Peter had the usual attempt at a few words. Da, da, ma, ma, baw for ball, and even bob, bob, for the immortal Sponge Bob cartoons he loved to watch. Just a few words were there to make a parent smile in anticipation of what was ahead in his world of communication.

At the age of eighteen months, things began to change for Peter. Instead of adding more words to his vocabulary, the few he had disappeared. For whatever reason, our child was changing drastically. As our concern grew, we brought in doctors and specialists to test and analyze him. By the age of two, we knew for sure that he was not deaf and that he definitely had delays in his motor skills and communication functions. Shortly thereafter, we received the official diagnosis of autism for Peter.

There is much I could tell you about this very difficult period in our lives, but instead let's focus on the communication aspects, or lack there of. Any parent of a special needs child will tell you that the greatest pains come in the world of communication. If your child is hungry, there is no way they can tell you. If he is inflicted with pain, he cannot cry and tell you where it hurts. If he wants his favorite toy that happens to be up on a shelf, you have no way of knowing why he is tearing down the wall to get to it. You can tell him you love him a million times, but the reply is only in his eyes, not on your ears. Instead of clear questions, there is screaming, moaning and animation. Many things get broken and many more will in the future as Peter attempts to tell us what he needs or wants.

In time, we, like any other parent, have learned to adapt. Peter's therapists have worked with us as well as him and showed us what certain gestures mean. In a world of leaps and bounds, we may not know what he wants to drink, but we know he is thirsty. We may not know what snack he wants, but we know when he is hungry. We may not know what toy he wants, but we know when he is looking. Autism has opened our eyes to a million non verbal ways to communicate and has made us sensitive to the world around us.

I have taken you down this path not only to share a very large piece of my life with you, but to show you how easy we can adapt to various forms of communication. Too often, in the world of customer service and business, we see the world in a two dimensional way. There are messages sent out by the company, by the merchant, by the service provider, and we receive them. If receptive, we reply back in a favorable manner. If non receptive, we reply in a negative manner or not at all. We see TV ads that make most of us laugh, while it makes other upset. In fact, there is a large segment of the population that does not get it at all because they cannot hear, they cannot read, or they speak a different language altogether. In all regards, the message does not go out to all.

As the world becomes a global marketplace due to advancements in technology and communication, the need for global base languages has risen as well. Universal symbols such as rest room signs and traffic signals have already been adopted all over the world. Sign language, although a slow movement, was recently termed one of the top five languages used in the world. In all, the signs are clear and evident. The earth's inhabitants want to break down the barriers of language and distance to communicate with each other. The magic of the internet has eliminated the distance quotient in communication around the world. The rest is up to mankind.

More and more often, when you contact a business, the recorded customer service messaging system will direct you to a number of language choices. More often than not, the larger the company you are doing business with, or the more global that company may be, the more language choices you will have. Unfortunately, not all companies have climbed aboard the global bandwagon. The longer they wait to open themselves up to communicating with more people, the further from success they will be.

In this new marketplace, savvy businesses know adaptability. They know that to not adapt will certainly mean failure. In urban markets, you will see one side of a company, while the billboard changes dramatically in the rural markets. In Hispanic neighborhoods, the advertising is in Spanish. In Chinatown, the language is Chinese. They do not have the audacity to place a billboard from an American company in the middle of Tokyo and cover it with English. Companies have learned to adapt their message to their audience, but many have not taken it to the next level and educated their people on customer service communication.

Any company that conducts business in the continental United States should have people on their staff that speak English. There is no excuse for any customer service less than that. The same holds true for any other country in the world. When I call Paris to arrange a seminar, I fully expect the conversation with the company I am calling to be in French. If that company has someone on staff that speaks English as well, then I am impressed that they care enough about their international business to have additional languages available.

Recently, I had some computer challenges and had to contact Dell Computers to straighten them out. My internal roadblock went on alert when I found out they were routing me to India to assist in my problem. I did not speak Hindu, so the conversation would probably be very short. To my surprise, the customer service representative that took my call spoke perfect English. Although I was doing business on a different continent, the rep made me feel completely at home.

*Whether you are conducting business on the phone, or buying meat at a deli counter, every customer wants to feel at home. They don't want to feel alienated in their local supermarket. They don't want to be treated as an outcast as they go about their shopping. Every customer wants to feel comfortable in their home language. The first rule in customer service communication has to be **stay true to the language of your customer.** The adaptation of this rule in daily business lies in the company itself. In America, speak English first. In France, speak French first. Simple rule, simple adaptation.*

Second, but equally important, companies need to give service in all languages. If you are doing business in American markets that also speak Spanish, then you should have people on staff that speaks Spanish as well as English. If your customers are Haitian, then there should be Creole speaking service reps. On a personal note, there should always be someone on staff wherever you go that can use sign language to communicate with your customers.

On a final note, customers are the reason companies exist. If they cannot communicate with them about their needs, their wants, their expectations and their complaints, the company might as well close the doors and pull up the stakes. If the customer and the company cannot connect, there is no business to take place.

6

Service With A Smile

Many years ago, I was a district manager for a department store chain in the northeast. During that time, I had the opportunity to encounter volumes of customer service issues in many of my stores. Some of them were more challenging than others, but none of them had the amusing flavor of the one you are about to read. In some ways, it has become the ultimate customer service experience, regardless of the origin of the customer.

As in many large corporations, the visiting process from upper executives can be a very stressful experience. To simplify, you put your best foot forward and hope that the people you depend upon the most come through for you. When I was a store manager, I vowed that if I were to be promoted, I would do everything possible to relieve that stress on my store visits. As time and God blessed me with that opportunity, I made sure I was true to my conviction. However, my actions could not prevent the stress when my upper management team came to town.

On a sunny fall afternoon, I was blessed to have the whole executive committee touring one of my stores. They were there to observe some of the new product presentations and see how customers were reacting to them in this market. The market in question had a reputation for being a low income based population, riddled with high shrink, or high theft store and today would be true to its legend.

As we toured the store, we encountered many customers. Families, individuals, young and old, a complete assortment of customers were at our beckon call. Of course not to be out done, every one in the group was eager to greet each and every customer and offer their assistance.

"Are you enjoying your shopping experience?"

"Do you shop at our store often?"

"Can I get that product for you on the top shelf?"

"Let me see if I can find another one for you in the back room?"

Each and every customer we met received the royal treatment from the top executives. It was a picture taking opportunity in an atmosphere most reserved for a political campaign. Filled with the good sentiment that was received from the customers and the employees at the store, our afternoon progressed well.

The entourage visited every aisle in the store until we completed the circle and arrived back at the front of the store. As we rounded the check out area, we observed a woman struggling to keep a large television on top of a carriage. The woman was heading for the front door and not one sales associate was offering assistance. The box rocked back and forth and was just moments away from the certain crash to the floor. Appalled at the level of service our company was offering this customer, the group had their call to arms and was ready to assist.

Upon first glance, three of the younger executives rushed over to the woman and assisted her with the box. They balanced the box on the carriage, opened the front doors and proceeded to carry the television out to her car. Seats were put down and parcels were moved aside to make way for the large television that her family would soon be enjoying.

The whole group of executives watched with pride as the store name was proudly being toted, with top brass getting hands on experience in customer service. With the television properly loaded in the car, the woman offered the execs a tip which they promptly turned down. The woman drove away and the beaming young lads entered back into the store with applause from the group. The applause was quickly cut off, however, as a small group of employees followed by security raced to the front of the store. The store manager and I promptly stopped them in their tracks to find out what all the commotion was about.

"Mr. LaPorta, have you seen a woman in her 40's come by here?"

"You have to be more specific, and please get to the point", I replied realizing that the eyes of the company were upon me.

"Well, this woman was back in electronics and we lost her, we think she stole a television, but we can't find her anywhere".

The group was frozen in their tracks. Could it be? Were we so quick to give customer service that we just gave our merchandise away? As we all looked at each other in disbelief we realized that the customer service we offered was to a thief and she was definitely satisfied with her transaction!

Who Hired (promoted) These People?

Afterthought

"The road to service is traveled with compassion and understanding...people don't care how much we know until they know how much we care"

"To err is human, to forgive, divine". Mistakes are made everyday under the umbrella of customer service because we are dealing with people. Human beings make mistakes. From the first days in the Garden of Eden to eternity, people make bad decisions. It's just a fact of life. All that you can do theoretically is to forgive, to correct, and to move on.

The fact of the matter is that it isn't that simple is it? If you are the one receiving bad service, it's not that easy to forgive and move on. It all hinges on what the service provider does in the situation. Service recovery can be a very complicated part of your everyday business unless you look at it in simple terms. Take care of the customer!

Guest service recovery is a term that is often used in the service industry. The term is used to describe an action that is intended to turn a bad guest service situation into a good one. The customer complains, you do some sort of recovery and the customer leaves happy. Simple enough, right? In theory it is very easy, however in real guest situations the recovery may not be that simple.

Let us first look at a simple restaurant situation where the steak you have ordered is delivered to the table. When you cut into the steak, you realize that it is very under done. In a trained instinct, you put down your knife and fork and call over the server. The first step at service recovery is now underway.

First Question. Is guest service recovery **necessary?**
Answer. Yes, unless you want to eat a raw steak.

"Yes, sir, what I can I do for you?"

"Well, the steak that I ordered medium is very bloody, can you have them cook it some more?"

"Certainly sir, I'm sorry. I will bring it to the kitchen and alert my manager. Is there anything I can bring you in the mean time? "

"Sure, maybe some more water, will it take long?"

"No, we'll make it a priority."

With that being said, the server turns and walk away. Your wife sits with her meal in front of her and asks if you want her to wait. You tell her to go ahead and eat since it won't take that long to bring it up to the right temperature. You sit and snack on the bread as you wait for your meal to return.

A few minutes pass and the server returns with your steak. This time the steak is extremely overcooked. As you attempt to cut into this piece of shoe leather, you shake your head.

"Oh, my. Is there a problem with your steak this time?"

"Yes. They scorched the steak. It's no where near medium."

"I'm sorry. Let me go get my manager."

"There is no need for a manager. I just need my steak cooked the right way."

"I know sir, let me get my manager."

The server turns and disappears as you sit with your wife and your overdone steak. The situation has now gone into the next stage of the recovery process. The situation takes a turn, however when the manager returns.

"Hi, I'm Bob; I understand we're having a problem with the steak."

"Hi Bob. Yes, we do have a problem. I ordered a steak cooked medium and it came out rare. When I sent it back it came out well done. I just want it cooked the right way. Can we do that?"

"Sure. Let me get another steak on right away and we will cook it right this time. And don't worry, I'll take it off your bill."

"I'm not concerned about the bill. As far as I'm concerned, I don't have a bill yet since I have yet to eat something. Can I just get my steak please?"

"Yes sir, I'll have it for you in an instant."

The manager leaves the table and the recovery process is in trouble. On one hand, you have no meal to eat. It is cooking, but after sitting at the table for an hour, you are back at square one. Your wife has finished her meal and sits patiently as you await yours. In anticipation, the manager has jumped the gun and given you the meal that you have not eaten yet, for free.

Is the recovery **appropriate?**

The attempt to re-cook the steak a third time is appropriate, but the mention of a free meal at this time is not. There has not been any food served to warrant a free check. If the check is to be cleared, then that action should occur at the end of the meal. This brings us to the third point of guest recovery.

Is the recovery **timely?**

If Bob did not return to the table right away, if in fact he took quite a while to come to the table, then the cooking of a new steak would definitely not be a timely action. At that point the recovery would probably not be appropriate either.

We return to the scenario as the steak returns to the table. At this time, your wife is completely finished with her meal and only awaits your meal to move on to the dessert course. Since Bob initiated this round of recovery, he is the one to bring your steak back to you.

"I hope this steak is much more to your liking. Please cut into it to make sure."

As your knife approached the cut of meat, you can feel the influence of Murphy's Law take its toll. The steak, of course, is overdone once again. The night is officially a disaster. Recovery from this point will be next to impossible.

"I can tell by looking at your steak that it's not right. My deepest apologies. Would you like another steak or would you like to choose something else from the menu?" (Appropriate choice, but completely untimely. The meal period ended a long time ago.)

"No, I think this dinner is done. Just bring the check and we'll be on our way."

"That won't be necessary. We have ruined your meal already. There will be no check tonight. Can I at least get you some dessert and coffee before you leave?" (Necessary, appropriate and timely)

"Yes, that will be fine. Thank you for picking up the tab. That wasn't necessary."

"No thanks needed. I will send the server over with the dessert menu."

Later, as you finish your dessert and coffee, the manager returns for a final visit.

"I know the dinner didn't turn out the way you planned it, so please accept these gift certificates for you to try us again. I assure you this was not our typical dinner service. Next time, we'll make sure everything is great from start to finish."

Is the recovery **relevant?**

Absolutely. The recovery is relevant because it completes the circle. It goes beyond the damage control and retains the customers as guests. By inviting them to return at a later date, the manager not only saves the situation, he possibly saves a guest. Whether or not the couple returns to the restaurant, it is very possible they won't have many bad things to say about the place. A second chance is probable for the future.

In review, there are four main aspects of guest recovery.

Is the recovery necessary? Has something happened against the customer that warrants some kind of recovery action? Will an apology suffice or does there need to be action?

Is the recovery appropriate? Are we offering a free trip to anywhere in the greater states because the stewardess spilled a drink in a lap? Overkill can make the recovery insulting and ridiculous.

Is the recovery timely? If a small child ruins his clothes from vomiting on an amusement park ride, will you mail a replacement shirt or give one to him right there? If the timing is correct, the rest of the day can be salvaged and the family can still enjoy the amusement park.

Is the recovery relevant? Do not offer a complimentary night's stay at the hotel because the guest didn't like their martini at the bar. People know when they are being taken for a ride and most people don't want to be taken anywhere.

In most businesses today, guest service recovery is fumbled. No one likes to admit fault. If there is something wrong, the answer must be user error or some outside force at work. If your cable goes out, it was nature's fault. If your plane is delayed, there was inclement weather. If you have to wait an hour to see the doctor even though you had an appointment, the doctor must have had an emergency.

For those companies that do embrace their downfalls, the recovery usually breaks one of the rules mentioned earlier. The credit for your cable being down shows up two months from now and you don't know what it's for. The restaurant tells you they will mail you out certificates for you to come back, but you never receive them. Such easy concepts, such sloppy follow through.

In summation, the easiest way to approach guest service recovery is to put yourself in the same situation and ask what you would want. Use common sense! If a child losses a balloon, he only wants another one. Nothing more is necessary. If you spill someone's drink, clean it up and get them another one. That simple.

*Above all, don't forget the most important words when something goes wrong. **I'm sorry**. Sometimes an apology is all a customer wants. If you give it immediately, it may soothe the situation completely. If you don't, the simple mistake may explode into a much larger one. So say you're sorry and mean it! You'll be surprised how much it will accomplish.*

7

SPEEDY SERVICE, FAST WHEELS, AND FOOD?

In today's restaurant industry, consumers have a plethora of eating opportunities. Full service, family dining, or quick service (formerly known to the world as fast food). Indoor table dining, outdoor patio dining. Cuisine from every custom on the planet find their way into our neighborhood eateries. In broad markets such as Central Florida, you could eat at a different restaurant every meal of the day, every day of the year, and never frequent the same one twice. With so many choices, it is a miracle how some places remain open, while consistently putting forth poor service or a low quality product.

As human beings, we are creatures of habit. We stop at the same gas stations, go to the same coffee shops, and eat at the same places day in and day out on our lunch breaks. Since time is limited, geographic location comes into play and the thousands of eating choices available in your city get reduced to a chosen few. When a new eatery opens within walking distance of the office, it is a guarantee that every worker will venture over at some point.

Recently, a new restaurant opened next to my Florida office with a new take on an old concept. Sonic Drive- Ins have been popping up all over the south in an effort to rekindle the 50's drive in popularity. They serve a basic menu of burgers, dogs, and malts and all the side items that go with the basic burger joint. Although a nice selection, it is not their menu that attracts many, it is the presentation.

Like a page from yesteryear, their restaurants are drive ins, which means that you drive your car up to a designated area and read your individual electronic menu board. You "call" your order into the main building where they process it. When the food is ready, a server brings your food out on a tray while they roller skate out to your vehicle. The tray is balanced on your car window and all transactions take place without having to get out of your air conditioned, music filled vehicle. If you are on foot, there is an outdoor eating area where you can basically get the same experience. All in all, this is a great revival of a classic concept, which should continue to fuel their growth.

Regardless of the niche factor, the new restaurant had an appeal to all my employees in that their front door was now approximately 100 yards away from our front door. You can't get more convenient than that without getting your food delivered. Once up and running, all of the desks in the office had copies of the new menu added to the daily lunch files. Whatever time of day, breakfast, lunch, or dinner, someone was found with a bag of Sonic food nearby.

Once all the hullabaloo of the restaurant opening had passed and they filtered through their first group of employees, the new neighbor settled into the same operational difficulties as most restaurants do. The door began its revolving process in recruiting, hiring, and training new employees. For every lunch that we ordered, a new person would bring it out for us. Shortly there after, the same turnover demon found its way into the management ranks and now there was never a familiar face.

One morning, while seeking some brain food for inspiration, I ventured next door for some breakfast. A favorite item on the menu was the toaster breakfast sandwich, composed of your choice of bacon, sausage, or ham, combined with egg and cheese, all on two slices of grilled Texas toast. I ordered my usual, which were a sausage sandwich and a ham sandwich to go. After waiting an average amount of time for the food and receiving it, I returned to my office to enjoy some breakfast.

The surprise of the day started when I un-wrapped the first sandwich. When the foil was pulled back I stared down at two pieces of bread. Not toasted, not grilled! Not even a hint of warmth besides the eggs and meat on the inside. Out of curiosity, I opened the second sandwich and was greeted by the same blanche of bread. But wait! Maybe I was given another customers order by mistake. Maybe someone ordered their food this way.

Being the optimist, I returned to Sonic with the food in hand and asked to talk to a manager. The young man who gave me my food to begin with said he was the manager, complaining that he was short staffed. Quickly explaining my dilemma, the manager apologized for the poor quality and returned a few minutes later with two new sandwiches. He offered me a complimentary beverage for my troubles, which I declined, being satisfied with the proper food.

When I returned to the office, I started the ritual again of removing my food and peeling back the foil. I was pleased to see that the Texas toast was actually grilled toast and proceeded to bite into the sandwich. The second surprise of the day was when I realized I was biting into bacon instead of the sausage or ham that I had ordered! After a few off color remarks being mumbled, I turned to the second sandwich and removed the foil. Grilled toast on the outside was a good indicator again, but this time there was no bacon. This time there was no meat at all, just egg and cheese!! Four sandwiches made, four sandwiches made wrong. Fearful of what would be served if I tried this endeavor again, I salvaged what I could and threw the rest in the trash. Enough time wasted on a breakfast sandwich!

As any typical consumer would do, I avoided the hundred yard dash to the Sonic Drive-in for a couple of weeks. I ventured to the usual haunts to fulfill my dining needs. Eventually the doom of lunch on the run caught up with me and I was forced to pick up a couple quick sonic burgers on the way to one of my seminars. As soon as the bag of food was given to me, my pedal hit the metal and I headed for the highway.

Once at a good cruising speed, I attempted to eat my lunch. I pulled the burger out of the bag and peeled back the foil. As I bit into the sandwich, I was immediately reminded of an old Blues Brothers song. In the middle of the tune, Jake asks Ellwood what a "wish sandwich" is. The reply is, "a wish sandwich is when you have two slices of bread and you WISH you had some meat, bow, bow, bow".

Yes, that's correct. A burger bun with no meat, wrapped in foil! How can this happen. How can someone be this busy or in such a rush that they forget to put the burger in the burger bun before they wrap it in foil? I'm sure you don't have to guess that the second sandwich was exactly the same way. What kind of cruel joke was this? I know I was overweight, but being forced to diet this way was ridiculous! It was a travesty of the American way of life. If a man cannot get a burger in his burger bun at a burger restaurant, how can the earth survive? If the youth of today are working in the burger joints across America, what will the future hold once they get older? In my crystal ball, I can only see French fry holders with nothing but salt, and milk shakes which actually have nothing but a cup of milk.

Who Hired These People?

Afterthought

"The character of any team is reflected in the standards it sets for itself."

Quality is job one. Without a quality product to put forward, there is no service to give. Too often, companies forget that basic premise. They get caught up in the hype, the marketing and the message going out to the audience. In their thirst for pole position, they forget to dot their I's and cross their t's. They cut corners, reduce budgets, and shorten their test periods. In the end they put forward a product that is below quality standards.

In the ultimate example of poor customer service through sub-level production, we look to the auto industry. With enough crooks to fill a penitentiary, this industry is notorious for selling lemons and lying about quality just to make a sale. In times of trouble, those with the least integrity seek out those lemons to increase their wealth.

Following the Katrina Hurricane disaster, the south was riddled with cars that had severe water damage. Surprisingly, these cars still had resale value. The dealers had ripped out the messy interiors, slapped on a coat of paint, and pushed the cars out onto the lots. In search of the ultimate deals, many customers thought they were getting a super bargain when they found these gems. Unfortunately, most of the second hand buyers knew nothing of the water damage under the hood. They visited their local used car dealership and picked out many "great buys". The new owners had no idea what they were in for.

Within months, engine problems started to pop up. Clogged fuel injectors surfaced everywhere because of the sludge in the gas tanks. Transmissions failed because of the amount of water taken in. Within a year, the paint jobs, started to fade and chip away. The truths were slowly uncovered but for too many, it was much too late. What little warranties the autos came with were long expired. For the owners, a hard lesson had been learned. Buyer beware!!

Far too often, the quality of a product is mysteriously hidden until long after purchase. Way down the line, a company puts out a memo that they discovered an issue with their product. They put out a warning. They call it a recall, and they expect it all to be ok. From the customer's point of view, it is far from ok. All of a sudden, the customer finds out that the product that they have been using for some time is sub standard. Sometimes, the recall brings up health issues, as in a drug recall. Other times, it brings up a major safety issue, such as an auto recall. No matter what service the customer has received before this point has gone out the window as the customer feels violated.

In the case of a drug recall, the customer or patient is instructed to stop taking the drug. Many times, follow up visits to their physicians as well as medical testing is required to rule out any future complications. More time, more money and more anxiety are the immediate side effects. After all is said and done, how does the customer feel about the drug company? Does the service they received from their doctor look any worse because of the discomfort they have been put through? Most likely, everyone that can be blamed, will be blamed.

Auto recalls and other product recalls can be just as invasive. How comfortable do we think the young parents feel when they find out the car they have been transporting their children around is defective? All of a sudden, after they have driven thousands of miles with their kids in the back seat, the vehicle is prone to flip over on turns. They start to play the should have, could have, would have game and their anxiety builds. Do they go out and buy another vehicle without driving another mile? Where do they go from here?

How safe does a driver feel when the tires they have been driving on for years are recalled? What about the appliance that is recalled because some models catch on fire? What's the reaction of the parent when they find out the toys that their kids use daily are recalled because they are hazardous to the kids that use them? All the confidence, all the trust and all of the good will associated with customer service are gone. Does the customer really want a replacement product from a company that allowed such dangerous opportunities into their safe home?

The initial resentment that a customer feels in any of these situations is nothing compared to those feelings that arise once the research is revealed. Reports roll in about injuries and tragedies and other terrible results. The customer then starts to realize that if the company took a little extra time in their planning and developing, none of this would have happened. If there was a longer testing period, they may have seen the long term effects. If the company would have taken more time to care about the quality in the first place, you would not be inconvenienced now.

If quality is job one, then why do companies put out a product that is not 100%? From restaurants to auto makers and every product in between, the end product has to be satisfactory to the customer. They make it for the customer, they sell it to the customer and they expect future sales from the customer. Why would they ever want to put a bad product out to their customers?

My father always told me to put my best foot forward. He also told me never to accept a wooden nickel. Later in life he warned me about buying a bad car (and the word lemon wasn't the only word he had for these). But in all the lessons he taught me about products and quality, the most valued one came from his life long work. For forty-two years he worked as a lathe operator in a machine shop. Day in and day out, the man created parts on his machines that were used in military and commercial aircrafts. From a monetary perspective, he was only paid on the quality parts that he produced. If he had a bad day and half his day he produced had parts, then he was paid half of his piece wage. Supporting his family, he could not afford to put out poor quality.

From a personal perspective, if he put out a bad gauge and it made it past the inspectors and onto the plane, the damage could be severe. If he did not take the care to produce a quality product, people could get hurt or die. His company would still get paid for the part and it probably would never get traced back to him. All would be fine except for two things; he would know and the customer would not be satisfied. On all accounts, unacceptable customer service, which he could not be proud of. That's why he spent forty-two years at the same machines making the same quality products.

8

ROOMS TO GO NOWHERE

One Monday morning, I asked one of my office employees how her weekend was. The look on her face was one of incredulity and amazement. I knew a classic story was about to unfold.

It seems that during the weekend, April and her fiancé were out shopping for home furnishings for their new house. In their travels, they stumbled upon the great furniture showplace, Rooms to Go. Although they provided a fine selection at their normal showroom, Rooms to Go had recently opened an outlet showroom to move some of their slower and discontinued items. This is where the young couple ventured to.

After what seemed like hours looking at various furniture selections, they decided to purchase a unique piece, which happened to be a mirror with various characters bordering the edges. As instructed by the price tag, they removed a portion of the tag and proceeded to the cashier to pay for their purchase. Once the currency had been exchanged it was time to pick up the mirror and bring it home. A simple request, you might think, but not at Rooms to Go.

"Sir, sir, what do you think you're doing."

"I just paid for this mirror, so I was carrying out to my car."

"You can't do that from the front door sir. Our rules state that all furniture must be picked up in the rear of the building."

"Well, I'm almost out the door now, do you really want me to put it down?"

"No, sir. I do not want you to simply put it down, I want you to put it back where you found it."

"Let me get this straight, even though I just paid for this mirror and I own it now, you want me to carry it all the way back across your showroom just so I can pick it up in the rear of your store?"

"Yes, sir, that is exactly correct."

After a few moments of silent meditation and restraint, April's fiancé, Doug, returned the mirror to the original spot. They exited the store and drove their vehicle to the rear of the store where they discovered a new world. They parked the vehicle in the designated parking area and proceeded up to a customer service window located next to the receiving dock.

"Hello, can I help you", offered the clerk at the window.

"Yes, here is my receipt. We need to pick up a mirror we just purchased."

"Certainly, let me make a copy of your receipt and we will send someone after it. Unfortunately, we are a little behind right now and it should take about an hour."

"An hour? An hour to pick up a mirror that I was just carrying out to my car myself. This is ridiculous, I'm just going to go in and get it myself."

As he left the window and approached the loading dock, the same clerk came out from behind the window and stood in front of him.

"Sir, I'm sorry but I can't allow you to do that. If you cross that yellow line I will have to have you arrested."

"ARRESTED!! For what? I'm just picking up a mirror that I already paid for. I am not going to wait an hour for someone to get it for me when I can pick it up myself."

"All I can tell you sir is that if you cross that line you will be arrested. Just take your copy and wait over there with the rest of the customers."

At that moment, Doug and April looked over to a little corral area where every other customer had the same disgusted and agitated expression on their face. April, being the cooler head of the two, pulled her fiancé away to wait with the other customers.

While they waited for their purchase to be brought out to them, the young couple observed customer after customer approach the window and view a similar sequence of events unfold. Each time a customer made a step towards the back door, they were threatened by police action. To their amazement, the most incredible part of their adventure was yet to unfold.

Waiting in the vehicle next to theirs was another young couple. The pick up truck they were sitting in was waiting to transport their beautiful new headboard for their bed. The headboard, a difficult find, was adorned with cut pieces of mirror that were arranged in a mosaic pattern across the top of the headboard. Keeping it all in place were two strips of ornamental mirror on the top and bottom of the headboard. As the time passed by, the couple shared that they had been waiting over an hour for their headboard to be carried out. As in every other case, the personnel in the store refused to allow them to pick up the headboard themselves.

Finally, the moment of truth arrived as two burly gentlemen came out of the dock carrying the headboard. As they approached the pick up area, one of the workers slipped. Apparently, the man was not watching where he was going and slipped coming off the curb. Unfortunately, the base leg of the headboard hit the ground and the impact caused one of the mirrored strips to come off and smash on the ground. In a realistic world, human error occurs. What happened next was something of a different sort. Although extremely apologetic, the two men did not skip a beat and continued in their loading of the headboard into the pick up truck.

"What are you doing? That headboard is broken. I need a different one."

"I'm sorry, sir, but since this is the outlet store you have to take the piece you pay for."

"I don't care what store it is. I'm not taking this headboard. You broke it and I want it replaced."

"Sorry, sir". With a turn and a shrug the two men left the headboard at the tailgate and returned to the store.

During the hour and a half that April and Doug waited for their mirror to be brought out, they observed the other young couple fight and argue with seemingly every worker at the store, including the manager. Although they were offered a piece of mirrored strip that they could glue on themselves, they were never offered a replacement for the headboard. Before they pulled away, April and Doug witnessed the final insult. With all other venues exhausted, the frustrated couple climbed into their pick up and started to pull away. Unfortunately, in all of the arguing, nobody realized that the lift gate of the truck was not closed. As the couple pulled away, the headboard slid off and smashed upon the ground. Through fist and fury, the couple looked back but continued to drive away.

The last thing April and Doug observed in their extensive afternoon was the two dock workers chasing after the pick up truck yelling at them to come back and pick up their mess!!

WHO HIRED THESE PEOPLE??

Afterthought

"Meeting people half way is the most significant trip we can take"

Compromise. Perhaps over time we have forgotten how easy and effective a compromise can solve a situation. Both sides bend a little and both sides come out on top. No losers, but a win-win situation for everyone. Unfortunately, some people and most businesses feel that there is no room for compromise. Their way is the only way.

Have you ever wondered who decided to put the postage in the upper right hand corner? Why there? Who was the first person to tell you that when you send a letter, the stamp goes there? What about the rest of the address label? I'm sure that someone told me the correct order of name, address, and then town and zip code, but I'm not sure who.

So, what happens when you change it up? What happens if you put the stamp in a different place? Being the eternal inquisitor, I've experimented a few times with this question. If you put the stamp in a different spot on the front of the envelope, it is still delivered. Depending where you put it on the front of the envelope determines if it will go through the automated process or not. If it doesn't, the odds are that it will just take longer for the envelope to get to its destination.

However, that's where the compromise ends. If you place the stamp on the back of the envelope, it gets returned for lack of postage. After three attempts with three different envelopes, I can clearly state that's where the compromise ends. If you go to the post office, the line starts over there. You put your packages here. Each package to be mailed has to be this big or this wide. It can't be more than this many pounds. You can't ship this or that and you definitely can't ship the other thing.

With the United States Post Office, there are not many compromises. Rules and regulations run abound from stamp size to package size and beyond. When customers demanded more services in a timely manner that the USPS would not compromise on, competition ensued. The formation of such companies as FedEx and DHL came about because there was a need. If customers cannot get what they want in the manner that they want, they turn to other avenues to fill their needs.

One thing that all of these companies will not compromise is safety. We often forget in our aggravation to ship our packages that certain things cannot be compromised. In order to protect other packages and people, we do not ship harmful chemicals or liquids. To protect national security, we make sure no firearms or explosives can be shipped. These are important rules and cannot be compromised.

In the auto repair business, there are signs everywhere that caution against the customer walking around in the repair area. So many things could go wrong that could cause harm to the customer. With power tools, chemicals, and large sharp objects everywhere, it is a cautionary nightmare with every step a customer takes in this area. Some repair shops draw the line and refuse to allow customers into their bay areas. Other companies, in a compromise to customer service, allow customers into these areas as long as they are accompanied by a mechanic or member of management. They seek to give the customer a higher comfort level by showing them exactly what repairs they are doing to the vehicles.

This simple premise carries over to other companies and other industries. For liability purposes, furniture stores cannot have you carrying furniture out of the store room. If you were to trip and fall and a sofa landed on top of you, what kind of liability suit would you have against them? If you were carrying a mirror and the mirror broke and sliced open your skin, who would be liable? *The safety and protection of the customer outweigh any inconveniences that may occur in an attempt to support customer service.*

During the interaction at Rooms To Go that started this chapter, the company would not compromise safety to make the customer happy. Although there were all sorts of mistakes made by the personnel there, the bottom line is that they were strict about their policies to protect the customer. They had a designated area for the customers to pick up their products. The area had a distinct starting point which was again uncompromised. In their eyes, they have to be strict or the customer gets hurt. This is a reasonable assumption in theory that seemingly is carried out in a totally unacceptable fashion.

The theme park industry is in a constant struggle to find a point where customer service is maximized without compromising safety. They set up a multitude of safety and surveillance equipment to protect theme park patrons from themselves. On the front side of customer service, they build roller coasters and attractions that will keep the guests thrilled and amazed. They strive to give the illusion of danger while in complete control of safety.

The engineers that build the attractions go back and forth on design. On one hand, they want every aspect to be themed, such as a roller coaster car with the design of a lion. On the other, the guests that get into that lion shaped car need to be safe. The lap restraints need to be tight enough to keep an excited guest in when the track goes upside down. The height of the car has to be short enough so that the guest can see everything while tall enough that they don't fall over the sides.

At what height can we allow the guests to be so that they are free of danger? If the allowed height restriction is at 42", can a compromise be made to get shorter guests on the ride and not upset them? How many families with small children get turned away because of height restrictions? Do they accept it or do they push the envelope? Are there arguments with the ride attendants? Do parents demand that their children be allowed to ride, even though it's not safe? The truth of the matter is that there is no compromise when safety is concerned. You can always meet a customer half way, compromising other aspects of the experience instead of safety.

The compromise in the safety restrictions at theme parks comes in a creative ticketing system that allows the parents to ride the attraction even though the kids cannot. One parent goes on the ride while the other parent waits with the children. When the ride is over and the parent exits, the other parent is allowed to go on the ride without waiting in line again. A win for the parents and a win for safety.

One final story is necessary to drive the point home. Years ago, Princess Dianna and her two young princes were visiting Central Florida on a vacation. Upon visiting the theme parks, they were treated like the royalty they were and compromises were made in every concession. They were escorted everywhere they went and were given first access to every attraction they desired to go on, waiting in no line.

A confrontation occurred, however, as the two boys failed to meet the height requirements on one thrill ride. The Princess urged the theme park employees to let them on anyway, but there was no compromise to be had. The political escorts met with the theme park managers in hopes of averting an international incident. The bottom line was drawn and the children were not allowed access. In the end the Princess understood that safety had to come before service, even to royalty. There were plenty of other attractions to go on and away they went. Each Prince was safe for another day, in hopes they rule their kingdom with the same compromise and integrity.

9

Our Policy Is.......

In the world of retail, there are many rules and guidelines that merchants follow in order to run their business. Some of those policies protect the customer, some protect the workers at the stores, but most of them protect the merchant against fraud, thievery, and an assortment of other unpleasant items that are all part of the traditional merchant system.

Pharmacies or drug stores are filled with such policies as they apply to not only the medical necessities but also the retail side of the business as well. Some protect the doctor, some protect the patient, and still others protect...well we're just not sure. One of my distant family members (who prefers to be just known as Jane in this story) had such an encounter at her local pharmacy.

One evening, Jane ventured out in the rain to pick up a prescription that she desperately needed. It was an ongoing prescription that had simply gone a few days too long on the refill and she was all out. She called in her prescription and the pharmacy had the medicine ready for her when she got there.

As she pulled up to the drive thru window, Jane stated her name and personal information and was told that her co-pay as usual was $10. Unfortunately for Jane, she had moved her checking account since the last time she was at the pharmacy. Since it was a newly transferred checking account, Jane had only starter checks with which to make her purchase. She filled in the check completely and handed it to the clerk at the drive up window.

The response she received was almost immediate and to the point.

"Jane, I'm sorry but we do not accept starter checks here."

"Excuse me?"

"Your check, ma'am. It's a starter check with no information on it, and I can't accept it"

"That's ridiculous", Jane replied. "I've been a customer at this pharmacy for years. My whole family has their prescriptions here. I'm sure you can make an exception for ten dollars!"

"Well, that is our policy ma'am. I'll have to get a manager to see if he will accept it."

For the next ten minutes, Jane sat in her car in the pouring rain waiting for the manager to arrive. Finally, a young man appeared and introduced himself as the night manager.

"Can, I help you ma'am?"

"Yes, I'm sure the young lady already told you but I will repeat it for you. I am trying to pick up my prescription, a medicine that I have been getting here for years. Unfortunately, I have just changed banks and I only have these starter checks to pay the ten dollars with."

"I'm sorry. It is our policy that we don't take starter checks. I'm sure you understand. Too many people out there writing bad checks to get free drugs."

"No, I don't understand. I have been a customer here for years. My whole family gets their prescriptions here. You have all of my information there in your computer including my medical history. It's just ten dollars, but I desperately need my medication."

"Well, Jane. That's our policy. I'm not going to take any starter checks from you. Do you have the ten dollars cash or shall I just return the medication to the pharmacist?"

"I am not going anywhere until I get my medication. I have a couple dollars in change. Let me have one pill for tonight so I can make it until morning when I go to the bank."

"No, Jane. I can't do that either. Our policy is that we will not split up a prescription like that. You'll just have to wait until morning, or whenever you can come up with the ten dollars."

"I am not leaving with out my medicine!"

"Lady, look, you either get out of my drive thru or I am calling the police."

"Fine, call anyone you need to but I need my medicine."

Unknown to Jane, the manager was already dialing the police department, complaining about an unruly customer in the drive thru.

Within minutes, the police arrived on the scene. They received the story from both sides and suggested the woman just go home. There was no compromise. Jane insisted on her medication. The manager insisted on her arrest and the rest of the night got uglier. Jane was taken away in handcuffs in the police cruiser. Her car was towed and impounded from the drive thru. Since it was late at night, she was unable to get out of jail until morning and spent the night in a cold jail cell without her medication.

The next morning, the stubborn night manager explained the incident to the General Manager. Then he explained it to the loss prevention people, the district manager, the regional manager, and the company vice president before all was said and done. Upon reviewing Jane's file, they realized that Jane was indeed telling the truth. Her family had shopped at the pharmacy for years. In total, her family members held sixty current prescriptions for a gross revenue amount in the ballpark of $15000 per year.

As news spread about the situation, Jane and all of her family transferred their prescriptions to other pharmacies. Jane was also a member of the local chamber of commerce and was active in the community. Everywhere that Jane went in the following year, she was sure to tell her story to. The local pharmacy became the local monster that preyed upon an upstanding citizen.

From the morning after to a period of six months later, Jane received phone calls from every department in the corporate pharmacy hierarchy. Apology after apology ensued. Offer after offer came in to try to heal the wounds. Jane would not budge. She would rather keep the hatred alive then give in to their apologies. With the damage done, Jane was a new person, and her whole family had a new pharmacy to call home.

Let's weigh the odds. Ten dollar starter check from a regular customer versus fifteen thousand dollars in revenue from her family and a community on the offensive. Tough choice.

Who Hired These People?

Afterthought

"A journey of a thousand miles begins with a single step"

Have you ever looked back to your high school days and wondered where all of those wild nicknames came from? It's not that these people introduced themselves as their wacky named counterparts. For the most part, It's a good bet that you can't remember the first time you heard them called that. Names like "Dollar Bill", "Two- tone Tom", or "Pennywise Perry", fill your memory banks with faded pictures. But were you there when they got those names? Who told you to call them that? If you saw them at a reunion, would you remember their real name, or has time embedded the nicknames?

When you get down to the root of the matter, you may or may not remember the answers to the previous questions. In reality, they probably all came about from a single episode with a small group of people. Perhaps it was a silly face made, or a not so smooth stumble; or perhaps it was just a foreign noise that came up that day. Whichever the happen stance, from that moment on, someone coined the phrase or nickname that would stay with that person. The next day at school, the new name filtered through the student body like a poison gas. Instead of just a few friends using the nickname because they were there, now everyone uses the name. Within a short period of time, the new name gets permanent status.

So, what happened? Dollar Bill never walked around with a name tag that made people call him that, the name just evolved. Much like the telephone game from summer camp, the name was just spread from person to person by word of mouth. Greg told Steve. Steve told Mike. Mike told Millie, and so on, and so on, until the whole school knew. When it comes to high school gossip, word of mouth is faster than a new e-mail on the internet. Can you imagine what would happen if it were bad news? How fast would the gossip spread then?

It's odd the things you remember in life. In the face of tragedy and terrible news, you often remember the messenger as well as the message. As a young child, I remember all the news coverage of the Watergate scandals, but I don't remember how I found out about the whole thing. Fast forward many years and I remember perfectly who told me about the Challenger disaster. I remember where I was standing and who I was with when Greg ran up and told me the news. Many years later, I remember with crystal clarity who told me about the 9/11 disaster and the number of people I told in the minutes that followed. It would seem that if the message is darker, it spreads like wildfire in the forest.

That being said, we can correlate the same message through customer service. Good news or bad, messages have a way of steamrolling. The old adage of spreading the word is monumental in the world of customer service. One of the most memorable phrases to come out of a commercial stresses this point.

"...she told two friends, who told two friends, who told two friends, and so on, and so on"

For a moment, let's look at the vacation industry. It is said that if a person returns from a memorable vacation, they share their experiences with 20-25% of the people in their interaction base. They flash their vacation pictures, tell huge fish stories about the one that got away, and perhaps mention a restaurant or two. In the end, they may carry away a story or two that might linger a while in the family circuit.

On the flip side of the coin is the family that has a horrible vacation experience. Before they return home, they have started the phone chain. No postcard can duly give justice to the horrible service they received on vacation so they cut to the chase. Without the physical evidence in the state, word begins to spread about the disaster at hand. With bad news to spread, 80-90% of the family's contacts are informed of their bad experiences. The rumor mill begins.

"Did you hear about Judy's trip to California? Her and John are on the way back but listen to this..."

"No really, it happened at an Outback Steakhouse..."

"Their Budget rent a car did what?"

When the family finally returns home, an angry mob of friends and relatives join together for the full story. Every aspect of the bad service is revealed.

"We stopped at a Sunoco gas station to get some gas and this slob named Harry came over to the car..."

"While we were staying at the Ramada in Norwich, this idiot named Robert was at the front desk..."

Facts begin to get thrown around and the incredible family vacation of 2005 becomes legendary. The gruesome details are shared at gatherings for years. The facts become distorted and instead of one gas station in the chain being bad, it becomes everyone on their trip. All hotels with the Ramada sign on the door become buildings of animosity. Every restaurant with an Outback logo becomes the feared eatery with bad service and overpriced food.

If the legendary family stories weren't damaging enough, every member of that family has friends, co-workers, and distant relatives of their own. As they travel to their social gatherings, the tale takes a life of its own. Like most urban legends, the wrongdoings escalate even further until each listener fears all guys named Harry.

"Let me tell you what happened to my in-laws..."

"You think that's bad, my cousin just got back from California and he got the worst service of his life."

"You know Susie in accounting? She just got back from a trip that the rent a car company ruined."

Like a sour bite of lime in the back of your throat, the stories leave a lasting impression. The words were strong enough to strike a nerve in each *listener. In time, a small incident on a family vacation can cause a company irreparable damage.*

"I know we have used Ramada hotels before for all of our company travel, but I hear bad things. Perhaps it's time to choose another chain"

"With all the problems I've heard Outback is having, maybe we should have our monthly meetings at another restaurant."

"Hey Harry somebody is taking over Sunoco. I hear customer service is not his priority. Why don't we move the company fleet to another gas provider."

Never underestimate the power of the people. With a single spoken word, they have shut companies down around the world. Remember, "A wave across the ocean begins with a single raindrop." The same holds true for customer service. All it takes to begin the chain reaction is a single act of poor service. One rude clerk, one late service technician, one night's stay at a bad hotel. The rest is up to you. Who are you going to tell?

10

COME SAIL AWAY, COME SAIL AWAY, COME SAIL AWAY WITH ME...

Let us take a journey. A journey that encompasses every aspect of customer service. A customer service experience that lasts from the first greeting to the bon farewell. Twenty four hours a day, for as many days as you sail aboard the ship. Every aspect of your senses will be attended to. A service provided for every whim. Our journey, of course, is in the cruise line industry.

Notorious for its service standards, the cruise line industry used to bring notions of grandeur. Voyages on vessels such as the Queen Mary (or may I mention the Titanic) bring visions of the elite, sailing on the high seas, with a server at their side every step of the way. We think of old world charm, of ballrooms and violins playing on every deck. We think of elegance and ultimate service. We also think of all of this in terms of yesterday and certainly not in the present tense.

Today's cruise lines have a mixture of that old world charm, but the most popular ones offer an endless supply of fun, adventure, and most of all guest service. For most people that have experienced it, they will tell you wild stories of their cruise experience. From the food to the casinos, the shows to their shore excursions, cruise lines provide you with a vacation unprecedented in any other vacation experience. As avid cruisers, my wife and I have experienced a multitude of different ships, crews, and destinations. Some, of course, are better than others, but two stand out in opposite directions as great examples in service. They also serve as a reminder that you get what you pay for.

On one end of the cruise example are the Carnival Fun ships. Having sailed with them many times from different ports, we have enjoyed a variety of offerings onboard. For my children, they have enjoyed the kids clubs, swimming pools, and an endless array of deck parties and activities. For Angel and I, the restaurants, clubs, casinos and spas have been the highlight of our cruising with Carnival. From the head of the household stance, the inexpensive cruises from nearby ports are perfect getaways for the family.

The Carnival experience has not always been ducky dandy. Our first experience was a disaster (although their guest service recovery brought us back for later adventures). It was a typical sailing for us from Port Canaveral, Florida, which happens to be an hour drive from our home and office. Our arrival was riddled with mayhem. The parking was much farther from the ship and more expensive than other ships that depart from the same port. To our amazement, it was cash only for parking so off to the ATM we went. This, of course, was no where near the port. Ok. Chalk one up to Murphy's Law and for our lack of preparation.

Once parked in our uncovered, marginally safe, parking area, it was time to move our tribe to the terminal. Although we had dropped the bulk of our baggage in the luggage area, we still had many carry on bags. With four kids and two adults, the amount of carry on bags can be overwhelming. Add to that balancing act the two little ones to carry aboard, it can be quite cumbersome. Luckily for us, there were no stewards or anyone else from the cruise line to assist in our long trek. Ok. No problem. We are seasoned professionals at moving this group.

Upon approaching the check in area, chaos ensued. With no accommodations for the children, they were expected to wait in the long line with everyone else. If any of you have tried to wait in a long line with an Autistic child, you are aware of the challenges. As a precaution, my wife or I usually approach a guest service person in these situations to see if any arrangements can be made before my son gets out of control. Unfortunate for us, the Carnival person we asked chose the wrong response.

"Excuse me, can I ask you a question? My son is Autistic and has extreme difficulties in crowded areas and lines. Is there a place that I could sit with him while the rest of my family waits in line?"

"No, get back in line."

"I'm sorry, maybe you didn't understand. My.."

"I said get back in line. Get out again, and I will call the port officials."

Fearing the kind of incidents that typically happen in airports, we got back in line. Today was not a day to have a conversation with the Department of Homeland Security. Needless to say, the next hour of check in was excruciating due to the lack of any concern from Carnival. Our need for a vacation was just amplified due to the poorly run check in process.

Amazingly enough, as we finished our check in process we were ushered into a picture taking area so that Carnival could take the first photos of our miserable faces. When we asked to pass on the photo due to our previous mood setting experience, the photographer insisted and therefore documented on film the emotions that we were all feeling. Sure, post that one in the viewing area!!

As in most cruises, once you are settled and go through the life boat drill, we were treated to a buffet spectacular on the top deck. When we arrived, the party was in full bloom with the band playing, the drinks pouring, and the atmosphere very festive. Finally, the journey to relaxation was right in front of us. Once we got the tribe fed, we could relax by the pool.

As our older two daughters found their way around the buffet, my wife and I started piecing together the smaller two lunch plates. With small children this can often be a challenge and today was no different. There was not a children's area set aside for their typical choices (i.e. Mac and cheese. Chicken fingers, etc). Having plenty of experience, we hunted down some items that could be cut down for their enjoyment and proceeded on. The main issue arose when we went to look for their drink.

Sara and Pete are no different than any other small child in their love of chocolate milk. They could drink it morning noon and night and never get enough of it. This is seldom a problem, since the world shares this fascination of this beverage. We have been able to find it around the world, even in remote locations. But today would be different.

"Excuse me; I see there is white milk on the buffet. Is there chocolate milk available?"

"No. No chocolate milk anywhere."

"Are you sure, can you check for us, please?"

"No, already checked. No chocolate milk anywhere."

"OK, what about chocolate sauce. I can mix it myself."

"Nope, none here. Check the dessert area." With that he walked away.

Upon locating the dessert area, the results were the same.

"No chocolate sauce today. Just fruits and pies. Would you like some?"

"Not right now, first I have to get my kids chocolate milk."

"No milk here, go to coffee station."

As the frustration builds, my search finds a viable alternative at the coffee station. Although we are sailing the tropics, there are packets of Hot Cocoa mix next to the tea bags. Go figure!! Chocolate milk can be made today!

Once through the lunch ordeal, we enjoyed the rest of the afternoon. The kids played and built up a good appetite for dinner. Although we were skeptical after the lunch quest, we were optimistic about dinner.

Dinner seating on cruises is typically quite the event. Service is usually extraordinary and the culinary creations knock your socks off. As another precaution for our son, my wife visited the Matre'D earlier and requested a remote location for our party. This usually takes care of any outbursts from Pete and ensures the other guests do not get disturbed.

As we arrived for dinner, we were led to our table in the middle of the dining room. When we asked about the seating, we were informed we could come back at the late seating and get a different table. With the clock ticking on and the children getting restless, we decided to take the center table and be the fish in the bowl for all eyes to pass judgment.

The wait staff was impeccable. They arrived at the table in a timely manner and immediately started their service. The bread came to the table as we ordered wine from the steward. All was going well until we ordered for the kids.

"A soda or juice for the little ones?"

"What they really want is chocolate milk, but I know you don't have any."

"What do you mean, don't have any? Of course we have chocolate milk. Would you like two?"

Our amazement went uncontained. How could they have chocolate milk now and not before? We have been out on the ocean. We have not stopped anywhere. While the server went to get the drinks, we fully understood. It was purely a service issue. The server up on deck simply was too lazy to go get the drinks. The two milks arrived a few moments later and we explained to the server about our earlier experience. He apologized and assured us that there would be plenty of chocolate milk the rest of our cruise.

The next morning at breakfast, we ran into the same rude worker from the day before. He was stocking the buffet a few feet from a mountain of chocolate milk containers.

"I'm sorry. Did you swim back to shore just to get the chocolate milk for my kids?" The joke just kind of slipped out.

"No, we always have chocolate milk! Shut up and move along. You are holding up the line."

Not to spoil the family vacation, I finished the breakfast line, finished eating and excused myself from the family. Quietly, I explained everything to the guest service folks on the lower deck and the rest of the cruise went as planned. The buffet server ignored us for the duration, but at least he wasn't rude. The whole experience was not cataclysmic, but it wasn't the cruise standards we were used to.

On the top end of the spectrum lies Disney Cruise Lines. Their impeccable service reputation around the globe holds true on the Disney Magic and the Disney Wonder. Having sailed both ships many times, I will simply take you through some highlights in comparison to the previous story.

Without exaggeration, if you have not sailed on a Disney Cruise you have not experienced true cruise service. Every detail has been thought of, planned out and executed a thousand times before you walk on the ship. Disney has thought of everything to make sure your voyage is unforgettable.

On a Disney Cruise, your experience begins in a couple different ways. If you are staying on Disney property in Lake Buena Vista, your transportation is provided to the ship at Port Canaveral. When you get on the Motor coach transportation, your bags are carefully checked and you will not have to handle them again. They will be placed inside your stateroom on the ship upon your arrival.

If your journey does not begin at Walt Disney World, similar services are available. You are directed to a curbside location where your luggage is tagged and brought to your stateroom upon your arrival. Your family can enter the terminal from there as you park nearby.

Inside the terminal, the Disney Characters entertain as you peacefully are guided by smiling faces through the check in process. There are even movies being played in the terminal to ease any tension that may arise. This time, as we finish checking in, we are excited and refreshed. The onboard pictures are full of smiles and anticipation.

Once aboard the ship, our family is treated like kings. The ships have everything you could ask for including movie theaters, kids clubs for all ages, and all sorts of activities for everyone. Our first day aboard is always an adjustment period for us as we detoxify from the outside world. With each moment aboard the ship, we are reminded of what true service can be.

Every Disney Cast member aboard the cruise is exceptional. With many cruises under our belt aboard the Wonder and the Magic, we have yet to meet poor service. The top service awards usually come from our wait staff in the wonderful restaurants. At dinner on the first night out, you encounter your wait staff for the first time. As your cruise progresses on different nights to different restaurants aboard the ship, the wait staff follows you. An excellent concept in guest service!

On one particular cruise, my oldest daughter, Amber, fell in love with a Caesar's salad that was served at the welcome aboard luncheon on the top deck. At dinner our first night, as the wait staff welcomed us and offered their unending service, my daughter mentioned this salad to the servers. Although not on the dinner menu, they assured her it would not be a problem.

As the wine and chocolate milks arrived at the table, so did my daughter's favorite salad. It seemed that the server had traveled to the restaurant on the other level and returned with her salad. She was elated. From that meal on, for the duration of the cruise, that server had her salad waiting for her at every dinner service. To take the service to yet another level, if she was not in the mood for the salad, the server offered to send it back to the stateroom as room service for her to enjoy later.

Service standards such as these are common aboard the Disney vessels. From the towel creations that the room stewards make in your room to the endless memories of the servers, your satisfaction is their only concern. Morning, noon, and night, smiling faces make you feel at home and never tell you to shut up. It begs the question…

Who Hired These People?

Afterthought

"Service is in the eye of the beholder"

Two boats leave Florida at the same time and travel to the same destination in the Bahamas. The will arrive at basically the same time and spend the same amount of time in port. While there, you will have the opportunity to go on the same shore excursions, visit the same points of interest and shop at the same stores. At the end of the day, you get back on the boat and enjoy the same basic amenities.

Both ships will have a fine dining experience for dinner. Both ships will have nighttime entertainment and offer nightclubs to party the night away. At the end of the night, you will enter rooms that are basically the same size with the same types of beds and comparable bedding.

In the morning the sun will rise over the same horizon, shining light to both the ships. If you go up on deck and look out over the water, you can actually see the other boat cruising along at comfortable speeds. The guests on the other ship seem to be having just as much fun as you are. They are swimming in the pools, sitting on the deck chairs, and drinking some kind of beverage like everyone around you.

Your day out on the ocean is filled with the same type of activities. There is shuffleboard, miniature golf, and skeet shooting up on both decks. Below, there are trivia contests, art auctions, and even a game or two of bingo. Food is plentiful on both ships and you can gorge yourself to you burst on delicacies galore.

As you look out over the railing at the other ship, you see someone back at you from the other ship. There is nothing out of the ordinary about the person. They are simply a guest on a different ship, on a different cruise line, having a complete different experience. As in a cross of destiny, the thought comes to both of you at the same time. Why is there such a difference in price? This is followed by yet another question. Why is there such a difference in reputation between the two cruise lines?

The answer comes in different fashions. On either side, the guests are immersed in their experience and they reply to themselves with prejudice.

"Look at him. What a fool. He paid twice as much for his cruise and went to the same place I did. I'm having just as much fun and I paid half the price. I win buddy, you lose."

With a little stretch of ocean apart, the other answer is skewed as well.

"I can't believe someone would sail with them. Sure, it's cheap, but it looks cheap. I'm sure they don't have the service like I'm getting here. Someone is taking care of my family 24 hours a day. I wouldn't trade it for the world."

Two families having very similar vacations, but their opinions are biased based upon the service experiences they are receiving. This concept holds true in every realm of the customer service arena. Whatever the product or service, consumers have choices. They exercise these choices everyday based on prior experiences and the service level they receive.

Every morning, people will travel out of their way to get a cup of coffee from Starbuck's or Dunkin Donuts. On their way, they will pass many convenience stores and other restaurants that serve coffee for a much lower price. Consistently, these consumers will pay ridiculous amounts of money comparatively to get a cup that has the Dunkin Donuts or the Starbuck's logo on it. Why? Some coffee drinkers will tell you that it is the taste of the coffee that is superior but many taste tests will argue otherwise. Quite simply, the answer is in the service they receive.

When someone pulls up to get a cup of coffee at a restaurant such as McDonalds, they are handed a cup with some cream and sugar in a bag and a coffee stirrer. As they drive down the road, they chance life and limb as they try to balance their cup and put in the ingredients that they desire. After this struggle is completed, they have to dispose of their coffee condiments and then they can drink their coffee.

When consumers pull up to the Dunkin Donuts drive thru, they tell the clerk that they want cream and sugar in their coffee. In return, they are handed a cup of coffee that is ready to drink, already mixed and ready to go. Is it worth the extra dollar or more? Many consumers say yes.

In the massive world of home products and repair, the giant retailer Home Depot has been king for many years. They offer a multitude of products under one roof and continue to dominate that market. For the past decade, however, their market share has been challenged by Lowe's. A carbon copy retailer with all the same offerings, Lowe's has been successful by focusing on one aspect. That aspect being customer service.

They began with making their stores less like a warehouse and more like a store that is aesthetically pleasing to the customer. From the lighting to the paint on the walls, they provide a more inviting showroom for which to shop. Once the showroom was complete, they filled the store with trained, knowledgeable associates that are available to answer questions, cut wood or glass, or simply to give you tips on lawn fertilizer.

In return, Lowe's prices are slightly higher than Home Depot's and there are not as many locations. Time has proven over and over again that people will travel out of their way to get that better service from Lowe's, even if they have to pay a little more. Customer service is their doctrine and their reward.

Whatever the industry, service is the deciding factor in the war of choice. In grocery chains, Publix dominates over chains such as Wynn Dixie purely on their service. Their prices are much higher than any other grocery chain and their selection much smaller, but they rule their market.

Walgreen's drug stores place service first and their consumers choose them over CVS, even though the latter has more locations nationally. Although powerhouses such as Wal-Mart offer the lowest prices on the planet, they lose a considerable amount of business to chains such as Target that place service before price.

Every day, in every corner of the earth, people have choices. They can go to one gas station or the one across the street. Same gas is pumped out so which one wins? When the product offered is the same regardless of which building it is housed in, the choice comes down to people. Will this person or group of people take better care and give better service than that group? Service is in the eye of the beholder. Choose wisely!

11

LESS SERVICE IS BETTER FOR THE CUSTOMER??

As you walk into the front door of the new Wynn Dixie concept store, you are instantly aware that you are not in your typical supermarket. Save-Rite is set up in some ways like a warehouse store, such as Sam's Club or BJ's. The food displays are not ornate with decoration or embellishment. In many cases, there are just pallets of food placed in the middle of aisles as if they had just rolled off of the truck.

In each department, the merchandise is stacked just a little higher than in regular stores, and the standard gondolas have been replaced with non standard warehousing bays to bring in more merchandise and presumably bring in warehouse prices as well. The general theme is well represented on the outer shell until you look deeper.

The first realization that the merchandising concepts aren't the only things that have changed is the personnel. There are very few people working in the whole supermarket. You don't find stock boys filling shelves or a produce man spraying his tomatoes. You just have an ominous feeling that you are truly alone on your quest to find the right groceries at the right prices.

A walk along the perimeter of the store brings great light to the new concept and its true business reality; save payroll dollars by eliminating customer service.

In the produce department, much of the individual produce items have been eliminated and replaced by full bags of fruits and vegetables. Presumably, these items have been packaged up at one of their other full service markets and brought over to display here in the discount market. Same items by their label, but you will not know until you get home and open up the bags.

The lack of service continues as you venture into what was once the floral section. There is no florist or flower arranger on hand to get you the arrangement you want or need. Instead there is now just a refrigerated section of pre-wrapped flowers and arrangements. Everything is nicely priced and easily accessible, but what of your special requests? Do you need five roses in a bed of carnations to signify a certain event in your life? No can do. No service here. What about some baby's breath to go with your roses, because your wife is particularly fond of that arrangement? Not here. Your requests would fall on the deaf ears of the cold cooler in front of you. No one there to give you service.

As you turn the corner, your belief in the grocery concept returns as you spy a deli counter with a live person behind it. But something is different. Something you can't put your finger on until you approach the counter. All the frills are gone. All of the frills that you come to expect in today's deli markets are not there in front of you. There is no area for the making of subs, grinders, hoagies, or whatever else you want to call them. No area for them simply because they do not make them. No need to waste service on a sandwich. Also gone is that wonderful glass case with all of the pre- made deli items we have come to expect. There are no salads of any kind. No roasted, broasted, or fried chicken. No chicken wings or French fries or chicken nuggets. There are no side dishes of any kind to compliment your meal. There is nothing there in the case because there is no case. Plain and simple. At this deli counter, you will find deli meat and cheese. They will cut it for you, weigh it for you and put it in a bag with a sticker. That is all. No frills, limited service. This must make someone very happy in the company not to overextend the service in this department!

In return, the deli department here has slashed prices, so they say. There are some savings off the regular supermarket chain prices. A quarter less per pound here, maybe fifty cents on another item, but certainly nothing to write home about and nothing to write about here.

Your perimeter walk of the store brings you through the meat areas next. Wynn Dixie, famous for being the meat people, have always delivered quality meat at reasonable prices. The meat department you encounter here is no different. Displayed the same way, with the same savings for larger packaging and such, the only difference once again is the service. They have eliminated that nice little window that you could bring your roast to and have the butcher slice up for you. There is no one on hand to split a large package up into little ones to make it easier to store and cook. If you need preparation suggestions or questions on the different grades of meat, you might as well pick up a cook book because there are no butchers available for any type of service what so ever!

As you complete your semi-circle shopping experience around the store, you come forward to the lack of bakery area. There are, of course, various bakery items available, but from where they came from is a mystery. There are no ovens baking fresh breads, but yet there are loaves of what seem to be bakery bread that has been imported from another place. Doesn't this technically make it vendor bread just like Wonder or Sunbeam? On yet another note are the birthday cakes and other prepared pastries. We are grateful for the opportunity to purchase such items, but how long have they been here? Who would write "Happy Birthday Angel" if I wanted to buy one for my wife? All the answers are lost in a void that we will just call "the bakery mystery of discount grocery retail"!

For the rest of the store, the aisles are laid out in a cross somewhere between a regular grocery store and a warehouse club. The shelves are stacked with boxes of items instead of just single units, presumably in hopes that you will stock up due to the extra savings. The great question exists on how much are you really saving. As a father and avid grocery shopper, the savings that are perceived are minimal and that is just not enough for everything I have had to give up in service to shop at this store.

The icing on the cake or the piece de resistance, comes to a point when you go to check out of this glorious shopping experience. You pull your cart up to the conveyor and place your items on the belt like any other food chain. The clerk proceeds to ring up your groceries for you and sends them down another belt towards the end of the chute. The service and your groceries all stop there. It is that point that you are responsible for placing all or none of your groceries into paper or plastic. If there is not another customer in the store, and no responsibilities what so ever, the clerk will sit back and watch you bag your own food items. You don't need to worry about squashing your bread or cracking your eggs due to mishandling; the only person left to blame is yourself.

On many occasions, I have personally come to the aid of the elderly of other fellow customers that have had difficulty bagging up their purchases. Whichever the case, the clerk has sat back and watched me with the look on their face that says, "Help if you want but I'm not going to budge an inch".

As you exit the store and head for your car, you wonder if there is a disclaimer posted on the door. If there is not, there definitely should be.

"Only physically and mentally capable customers should enter or exit these premises. We are not here for customer service; we are only here to take your money. Do not ask any questions, for we have no answers. Do not ask for any service, for we will give you none. In return, we have dropped our prices a few pennies. Enjoy the savings"

Who Hired These People?

Afterthought

"The customer is not here for us, we are here for the customer"

Everywhere we look these days, people are losing out to the two word term "self- service". I'm not exactly sure where the movement started but I have a good idea that it began at the gas stations around the country. I can remember with crisp clarity, when I was a kid, going to the gas station with my dad.

It was an experience that people poke fun of in movies such as "Pleasantville" or even "Back to the Future". The gas station attendants would come out to your car and greet you in their uniform (yes, I said uniform). Whether it be a coverall and a cap, or in the latter years a shirt with their gas station symbol and their name sewn in at the pocket, they came up to your car with a smile on their face and a clean rag in their hands or pocket.

"Fill it up Ted", my dad would say, and the whole experience began.

First, Ted would go around to the rear of the vehicle, pull down the license plate and unscrew the gas cap, placing it on the trunk within a rag or up on top of the gas pump. Without asking, Ted would come up and start washing the windows of the car and strike up a conversation with my dad. The clean rag would come out as he wiped the residue of the window squeegee and proceeded to clean around the whole car. The process never failed as I watched my father pop the hood of the car as Ted went to finish the rest of the windows. It was the unspoken lore of the road that the attendant would then check your fluids under your hood.

"Down a quart, Tony" or *"You could use some more anti freeze"* always brought some small pleasure as the service ritual would continue a while longer. Upon request at some stations and automatic at others, your tires would be checked for proper inflation, with free air dolled out without a second thought.

"You're all set Tony. That will be ten even". The exchange of money would signify the end of the transaction but not the end of the service. As the attendant walked away, he was sure to quick wipe with a clean rag any fingerprints he may have left behind on your cars exterior. A comical gesture in the eyes of a child, but a bit of nostalgia to these aging memories.

This ritual was the same throughout the country. Sure, there were variations on the theme and sometimes a team of gas station attendants would service your vehicle. Whatever the case may be, the number one rule of all theses filling stations was service. The more customer service that you could doll out to the patrons, the more business you could generate through word of mouth.

"Hey, Ted's station just started washing your tires while you wait".

"That new station up on Route 66 has three guys working on every car"

Then one day, the world woke up and it had all slipped away. Where were the service stations? Where were the attendants? Where were the green stamps given away with fill ups? Where were the free sets of steak knives and free collectible glasses that were given away just for getting gas in your vehicle? They were replaced! With what, you ask? The answer is all around you on every corner in America. The great America service station was replaced with self service gas stations and convenience stores.

Somewhere, someone got the great idea that you should pump your own gas. You should be able to do it. It's not that hard. Ask most children these days even in their pre- teen years and they can explain in detail how the process works.

Now, you park your car in front of any of the many gas pumps at the local self service station. You shut the car off and get out into whatever weather mother nature has decided to send your way today. You open your gas cap, stick the nozzle in, choose what grade of gas you want and begin pumping. Depending on what time of day and whether or not the gas station owner trusts his customers, you may be required to pre pay inside or pop out the old credit card and pay right there.

If you want to wash your windows, you do it (as long as no one has stolen the window squeegee this week). If you want your oil or any of your fluids checked, pop that hood and get to it. Didn't read the manual? No worries, no one around to help you in any way. If you want air, pump it yourself, after you pay for the air! Need your wipers checked? You have a better chance of seeing Moses. Take it to a mechanic.

If you hunger for a bit of nostalgia, you can travel to the great state of New Jersey where at press time it is still unlawful for you to pump your own gas. There are still guys that come out and take care of at least some of the items that have been listed already. Unfortunately, I can't guarantee that they will smile while doing it because the world just isn't the same place anymore.

The world of self service gas is just the tip of the iceberg. We are surrounded in every direction by the self service ideal. In the banking *world, we have the ATM where we do our banking at any hour as long as we are brave enough to watch our backs while doing it. If that doesn't thrill you, the banks let you serve yourself with online banking our even over the phone. Any and all steps have been taken to ensure there will be no customer service given to you.*

The internet has unveiled seemingly unlimited potential in taking away customer service. There, you can shop for a car, order flowers, buy postage, balance your business affairs, even shop for a future wife or husband. You want medical advice, don't bother with a doctor, find your answers online. You need cooking lessons, no class needed with a teacher, just look it up online. If you are in true need for customer service, no problem. I am sure there is a computer operator somewhere in the world, waiting at a keyboard for your question to come across their screen.

In conclusion, there should be no shock in the supermarket concept that Winn Dixie put forth. In this self service climate, new concepts of self service are everywhere. If you don't have time to go to the supermarket, there are stores currently available where you email them your shopping list and they will gather up the products, package them together, charge your credit card and deliver them to your door. At least in that example they are providing a service to the customer not taking one away. If there was a problem with the charges to your credit card, don't fret. The bill wasn't compiled by a human being, just a computerized scanning device that scanned the whole cart on the way out. No one to give service also means no one to yell at if there is a mistake. Seemingly a win- win for everyone. Or was it a lose- lose? You decide.

PART TWO

LIGHTENING ROUND

12

Every person on the planet that has contact with others has some sort of pet peeve about customer service. It may be the newspaper boy, the girl at the market, or a company's phone system. In this day and age, the possibilities and complaints are endless. However, to give each of those gripes their own chapter would mean certain death by length for this book, and you the reader would tire of the stories.

As a peace offering, I give you these quick outtakes for you to place your own story in. Enjoy!!

- If they call it a customer service hotline, why is there no one live to speak to? Just a series of voice prompts....

- Why do the meanest people with attitudes always end up working the customer service desk....

- To buy insurance, press one to speak to a salesperson; to file a claim, press two for forever hold....

- The wait time at the EMERGENCY ROOM is always so long!! Why would you go there unless you needed to be seen right away....

- Why are the most popular sale items never in stock during the sale? Don't the retailers want to serve their customers product....

- Why do you still have to show the attendant your card and id if you choose to pay out at the gas pump?

- Why bother printing your address and license information on your checks if they still want you to show them both to you at the time of purchase?

- The check out clerk who is talking to everyone else but YOU, the customer, about her break, her boyfriend, her hair, her nails....

- The check out girl talking on the phone to her friend about her break, her boyfriend, her hair, her nails....

- The check out girl who COMPLAINS to YOU, the customer about her break, her boyfriend, her hair, her nails (Who cares)....

- The waiter who has to sit down next to you to take your order....

- The waiter who comes back to the table three times to get the order straight....

- The waiter who complains about his tips....

- The waiter who counts his tips in front of you...

- The waiter who chews gum while he takes your order....

- Any customer service person who chews gum in front of you...

- The clerk at the store eating their food as they try to ring you up (oops, sorry about the jelly on your card)...

- The daily newspaper that always ends up anywhere but in your driveway or the front step...

- The Sunday paper that ends up in twenty different parts of your yard...

- The bartender who can never make the same drink the same way twice...

- The bartender who thinks they are the Da Vinci of the cocktail world and changes every drink recipe just to be creative...

- But this drink was two dollars less yesterday...

- "Sure, I can fit you in. The next appointment open for the doctor is in six months, is that OK?"

- "I understand you have medical insurance, but the doctor does not want to wait for his money. You'll have to pay the total bill today and we will refund the money when the insurance check arrives."????

- So let me get this straight, you want me to pay how much just to guarantee that the post office can deliver this in a week?

- The one single line at the post office for every transaction under the sun, that never seems to move...

- The eight lines at the tax office and whatever line you get in is the wrong one...

- The four lines at motor vehicles and every one of them is the wrong one...

- Six special coffees of the day, are any of them just plain regular coffee? Of course not...

- The amazing game of trust at the local dry cleaners, sometimes you win, sometimes you don't, sometimes we find your clothes, sometimes we don't...

- The photo lab that requires you to pay for all of your photos whether you are happy with them or not...

- The one hour photo lab that says it's just a catch phrase, not a guarantee...

- No, we used to be fast food, now we're just fast service and the food takes a lot longer...

- "We can be there on Tuesday between 8am and 5pm"...

- The cable programming that gets knocked out every time it's raining, oh yeah, sorry about that important show (sorry, no credit on your bill, either)...

- Free minutes, those are only good after 11pm, which is perfect if you work the graveyard shift...

- Free towing for the first mile, arm and a leg for every mile after that...

- Free delivery on every sale. We can fit you in next month, unless of course you want to pick it up yourself, then you can get it today...

- Free legal advice; oh no, we can't talk about that you'll have to see a lawyer for that one...

- Free medical clinic, open second Wednesday of every

month 10am-2pm, all other times, see your local doctor or hospital????...

- Buy one get one free- sorry we only have one in stock…

- Yes, we did use your 10% off coupon, but we also added in an automatic 18% gratuity (before your discount of course)…

- The chicken restaurant that stays open until 11pm but doesn't make any more chicken after 9pm…

- "We offer a special carpet cleaning service at $7 per room. If you want us to use any cleaning solution, however, that will be $40 per room???????"

- Having to pay for the shopping cart before the department store will allow you to use it.

- 32 cash registers and only three of them open???

- The waitress that drops the check when the food comes and you never see them again.

- The hotel rate is $50 tonight but changes to $150 for the next two nights. Same room, right?

Who Hired These People?

PART THREE

THE CHAMPIONS

13

As an eternal optimist, it would be against my grain to simply zone in and highlight all of the bad hires in customer service. On a daily basis, there are millions of people out in the world that their sole purpose is to give outstanding customer service. They certainly outnumber those who do not care about service, although some days it seems the other way around.

The companies that hire these people are the true champions of customer service. They instill customer service in their work ethic, and breed it in their employees from beginning to end. For some of them, there is no substitute for exceptional service. It is job one. If you cannot fathom this basic principle, then do not bother to apply.

For that same optimist, I am sure that there are thousands of companies out in the world who hold these beliefs to be sacred. Although I consider myself to be worldly, I am sure that I have only begun to scratch the surface of these outstanding people; just as I am equally aware that the losers mentioned earlier are a microcosm of those that deliver poor service daily.

In the pages that follow, I would like to take time to point out a few of the companies that have really knocked me off my feet as far as their approach to customer service. I not only honor them in each story, but I make it a point to mention them during my seminars and keynote addresses. This secondary tribute amounts to the thousands of people I speak to each year. In this framework, it is far better to be revered as a champion of customer service rather than a loser. The book therefore takes on a different meaning to the title...

WHO HIRED THESE PEOPLE?

14

THE BEST TRIP TO THE GROCERY STORE YOU WILL EVER HAVE...

To call them a grocery store is to severely understate their purpose on this planet. They are the ultimate shopping experience from young to old. They are an entertainment, an escape, an afternoon out, but never just a place to stop and pick up a quick gallon of milk. They are the place to have your child's birthday party or a place to take your kids to see animals. You take hayrides there in the fall and take in all of New England's majesty. You go see Santa during the holidays and take a sleigh ride while you sip hot chocolate. During the summer months you take in a barbeque or a clam bake under the big tent. You buy your pumpkins there in the fall, your wreaths and trees in the winter, your new bed of flowers in the spring, and all of your summer cookout needs in the hot months. There is truly no place like **Stew Leonard's** on the face of the Earth and no customer service book is complete without them.

Although a tiny dot in the world of mega- grocers out there, Stew Leonard's is the king of customer service. With just a couple of stores located in western Connecticut, you might be questioning why even mention them. However, among the many customer service books I have read over the years, there always seems to be a blurb about this amazing company. Executives from all over the world fly into Danbury and Stamford Connecticut just to experience first hand the unequaled sense of customer commitment and loyalty as a direct result of Stew Leonard's service.

To fully understand the experience, allow me to take you on a tour of the mind. Whichever store you choose, whichever your approach, your senses come alive while on the approach to the giant complex. At first glance the building resembles a very large barn with many things going on outside. As you drive in from one of the entrances, you pass the outdoor petting zoo, complete with goats and sheep and all of the expected fare. The parking lot pulls you around past the loading area for the hay and sleigh rides.

You pass the nursery where the change of seasons brings your choice of outdoor shrubs, trees and flowers.

If you park your car on one side of the building, you are treated to a view of their amazing birthday center good for any size gathering. On the other, you walk past their outdoor concession area which changes according to the season; at one point a clambake or barbeque, and yet at other times a great place to get some hot chocolate.

When you reach the front doors, you are instantly hit with the reality that this is not the average grocery store. Etched in stone at the entrance to the store are Stew Leonard's rules of thumb.

Rule Number One: The Customer is always right.

Rule Number Two: When in doubt, refer back to Rule Number One.

Not just a paper sign tacked on the wall. Not a clever advertising slogan on a hanging sign. A huge slab of rock right at the entrance proclaiming that you have come to the right place to shop and you will be treated right.

As you move past the stone formation, your senses take in a variety of activity. In one direction is a coffee shop. Whether it is a quick cup of Joe to aid you on your shopping mission, or an espresso to share with a friend at one of their café tables, the choice is yours. On the other side is a creamery full of fresh made ice cream products and treats to tempt even the most discriminated pallet. If it is simple New England refreshment that you need, barrels of fresh apple cider adorn the walk way so that you may sample at your free will.

Your journey continues into a maze like formation which will direct you through the wonderful store. The next area you encounter is the bakery as the sweet aromas fill the air. As opposed to most stores who give out their broken cakes or cookies for you to sample, at Stew's, they want you to sample only the best. Whether it is whole cookies or possibly mini muffins, your taste buds come alive with the possibilities. On hand in the bakery, as in all the various departments, are personnel waiting to answer any questions on food, product, or presentation that you may have.

The journey through the various areas is one of enlightenment as you realize that it is the small things that distinguish this store as great as opposed to others. In the seafood market area you encounter a demonstration and sampling of how to prepare and serve various fish. Not to be outdone, the demonstrator prepares not the low end, but such dishes as salmon, lobster, and crab. They tie the experience together by showing you what sauces, side dishes and even wines go with the food choice of the day. The presenter is not an extra person hired simply to doll out the samples, but a trained employee, armed with the knowledge of all the seafood offerings in the store and the ability to prepare them.

In the meat department, the service escalates to yet another level. Butchers are on hand not only to answer your questions, but to be your personal meat valet in your steak of choice. Choose a whole New York strip and you will be asked the thickness of steak you prefer, fat content, and how you like to prepare them. Would you like your steaks wrapped individually or collectively? Choose a sirloin butt and your choices continue. Filet mignon? Not a problem as these skilled professionals cater to even the most discriminate shoppers. If you're not sure on how to prepare the filet, you can always ask the butcher or step to yet another presentation area where filet mignon is being prepared and sampled out to the shoppers.

In addition to the basic departments, all of the extras fill your shopping experience with pleasure. Throughout the store, various animated figures entertain and delight your children. In the dairy section, a talking cow brings out the giggles. In the packaged goods section, the Hostess Twinkie talks and delights all who walk by. The egg section would not be complete without the animated chicken going about the egg producing efforts. Your food education is enhanced in the dry goods are as fresh soup is prepared and served. Not sure how to make a soup from scratch, simply ask the employee working the counter. They will provide you with a recipe and tips to change the basic make up to fit your dietary needs.

As your shopping journey approaches its final leg, you encounter the icing on the cake. If you are too tired or time crunched to cook the food you have chosen today, step up to the restaurant area of the store. In this section a pizzeria along with a full buffet area provide you with many delicious selections. Purchase a slice or the whole pizza. Choose chicken legs or whole chickens to serve to the family. The choice is entirely up to you. If you want some information on how to prepare any of these dishes, simply ask one of the employees and they will be able and eager to assist.

The indoor experience comes to end at the checkout area where courteous, knowledgeable clerks take care of your selections with care. Instead of candy lining the impulse areas by the register, your choices are a little healthier as fresh flowers are available for the adults and balloon selections for the kids. Your purchases are bagged and placed into your shopping cart with care. If you need assistance getting the bags to your car, able hands are just a request away. As you exit the store into the parking area, your choices begin again with all of the outdoor activities Stew Leonard's has waiting for you. If nothing else, add to the smile on your face by visiting the petting zoo or taking a hay ride. It will be an experience you will not soon forget.

Who Hired THESE People?

15

THE PHARMACY AMERICA TRUSTS

Business analysts say that if a new company can endure the first five years it has a fighting chance. Once that business crosses over the ten year mark, it is said to have been established. If that same business can somehow reach the twenty five year mark, then it has found itself part of the community, whether that means local or global it depends on the company.

There are very few companies that have been able to endure a century. With the United States itself only celebrating a little over 230 years old, it is unheard of that a single business could endure the 100 years mark. After all, during the last century we have endured two world wars and countless other world battles. As consumers, we have seen a revolution of products and services during that time. Such a company would have served not only your parents as children, but your grandparents and in many cases your great grandparents. Such a company would have to be solid in its values and steadfast in changing with the times.

There are only a handful of companies that fall into the category described above. At the top of mind, most people think of companies such as Coca-Cola and Kodak that have been around for over a hundred years. Fortunate for both of those companies, they have survived through all of the world hardships in partnership with yet another company. The stores that provided a shelf to these giants of industry through all of those years is Walgreens Drug Stores.

Walgreens was established in 1901 by a pharmacist named Charles Walgreen Sr., and has since endured well past the 100 years mark. With his mind set on service and dependability, Charles built a pharmacy dynasty that has since blossomed all across the country. Since the early days in Chicago to the countless cities of today, Walgreens Drug Store prides itself in customer service and has made numerous contributions to the world of retail.

In his very first store, it is said that Charles Walgreen enjoyed playing service games with his customers. As legend would have it, Charles would take a phone order for a prescription and keep the customer on the line while he filled the medicine. As he fumbled through the phone conversation, he handed the prescription to his delivery boy and put him on the run. Often times, the customer would have to excuse themselves from the phone as they went to answer the door for the delivery. Now that's what I call service! Imagine how successful a company would be today if they could deliver that type of service!

As the years passed, the innovations from Walgreens continued to mold the customer service model. In the early 1910's. Walgreens was one of the first drug stores to place the infamous phone booths in the back of the store. In this strategy, they guaranteed that customers would have to walk past the merchandise displays going back and forth through the store. In time, those booths were banked by the pharmacy soda fountains that changed American culture.

The drug store malt shop was born and Walgreens was on the corner. Soda, ice cream, and coffee all served at a counter while customers were making purchases all around you. The traditional soda fountain concept became the rave of America and soon made their way into all of the Walgreens Drug Stores.

To provide his customers with shopping choices, Charles Walgreen had the idea to create his own products to rival the more expensive brands. As Walgreens churned out the first store named products such as ice cream, candy and chocolate, the first generic products were born for the customer. Today, they offer thousands of products in their stores with their logo on it.

The number of customer innovations in the Walgreens Company seem to have no end. Where would a hamburger and fries be today if they had not invented the malted milk shake at the Walgreens soda fountain in 1922? How would businesses improve their customer service standards without the inception of Mystery Shoppers by Walgreens in the early 1930's? The list goes on and on.

Walgreens embraced the war years while maintaining service on the home front. The continuance of the staffed cosmetics department is still a rarity today. They pushed the envelope when they partnered with their old ally Kodak in developing one hour photo locations in all of their drugstores, providing yet another service to their customers. Breakthrough after breakthrough, Walgreens has spent over a century pushing the envelope for every one of their customers.

All technical endeavors aside, Walgreens became the envy of all with two customer service inventions later in the century. First, Walgreens pioneered child proof caps on all of their prescriptions long before laws came out the required them. Words cannot express the amount of lives that have been saved through simply restricting access of harmful drugs. One simple idea with a lifetime of implications.

Second, someone at Walgreens came up with the amazing idea to have a drive thru pharmacy. In practice, this service was designed with the customer in mind. If you are sick and need a prescription, why would you want to drive to the pharmacy, drop off your prescription, wait in an area with plenty of other sick people, and finally receive your prescription some time later?

Walgreens designed a method that relieves all that discomfort. The process begins as you pull up to the drive up window and drop off your prescription. The friendly tech takes your information and gives you a time to return for your completed prescription. When you return, you simply pay for your medicine and drive away. In many cases, you can phone or fax over your prescription and it is waiting for you as you drive up to the window.

Many variations of the pharmacy drive thru have been copied by rivals, but Walgreens maintains a full service environment as the pioneers for this service. As time rolls by, they add plenty of variations to the drive thru experience. While very few banks still give out lollipops to all the kids coming through, Walgreens gives them out at all their stores. To go one step further, if a car pulls up with a dog in it, the pet receives a dog biscuit! Wow, talk about looking out for every member of the family!

Although I've presented many of the services that Walgreens has adopted over the years, it's just the tip of the iceberg to the offerings in their stores. With many of their stores open twenty four hours a day and on every holiday, they are there when you need them. They offer services in fourteen languages. They add flavoring to kid's medicine to make them not so yucky. They are the place to go every year when you need a flu shot and they are always available for a prescription consultation.

On the horizon, Walgreens is finding new ways to serve the customer better. In many of their stores they are bringing in variations on the soda fountain with a concept they call Café W. The basic premise of enjoying a hot or cold beverage while you shop is still there; it's just packaged differently.

To take care of their pharmacy patients, Walgreens is installing walk in clinics in many of their locations. If the customer is ill, they simply pop into one of these clinics and they can diagnose the condition, write a prescription and fill it in one stop. No driving from the doctor's office to the pharmacy, no long lines, and no misunderstandings on the prescription. One stop shopping. .

In the front of their stores they are pushing the envelope literally by providing shipping services through DHL. Many locations are adding DVD movie rentals and their photo labs are expanding into the digital age. As the world changes and the service needs change, Walgreens is there on the cutting edge.

For over 100 years, Walgreens has been providing unparalleled service to its customers. Their partners in service, Coca- Cola have been in business for 120 years, Procter and Gamble at 171 years, and Kodak at Kodak for 127 years. With that kind of experience at taking care of their customers, why would any customer not want to shop at the pharmacy that brings them all together under one roof. The Pharmacy that America Trusts is Walgreens, for service and so much more. My pick for hero of the pharmacy business.

Who Hired These People??

16

THE GOLDEN ARCHES OF SERVICE

Lunch on the run. We all take it for granted. A meal that is prepared in a matter of minutes, so that you can consume it in a few more minutes and get back to the rat race treadmill. For years, the world has called it fast food and why not? Regardless of what you order in these establishments, it is prepared from start to finish in a matter of minutes. In most cases there is meat, vegetable and a starch prepared at lightning speeds for you the consumer.

Recently, the fast food phrase has been replaced with such labels as "quick service". The restaurant people want to focus on the quick service they give you rather than the fast food that they serve. But the two are synonymous in this industry. Quickly cooked food served at a rapid pace is what every fast food restaurant strives for. Where did they get the idea? From the leader of the pack; the one and only McDonald's Corporation.

In 1954, a man named Raymond Albert Kroc became fascinated with a device called the Multimixer. It allowed five milk shakes to be made at the same time on the same machine. Understanding how many customers could be serviced at that pace, Ray knew he had discovered a gold mine. He mortgaged his home and sunk his life savings into becoming the exclusive distributor of the machine. At the time, Ray was 52 years old.

A salesman to the very end, Ray always looked for ways to expand the business. When he first heard of Dick and Mac McDonald's Restaurant in San Bernardino, California, he could not believe his well fortune. The two brothers were operating eight of the Multimixers at one time. That would be forty customers getting shakes at once! With a head full of ideas and a sense of curiosity, he packed up his car and headed to California.

When he pulled up to their restaurant, Ray could not believe his eyes. Never before had he seen so many customers serviced so quickly. Switching to sales mode, Ray saw dollar signs if he could convince the owners to branch out and build more restaurants. Every one, of course, would need to be outfitted with eight of his Multimixers. Not swelling with the entrepreneurial spirit, the McDonald brothers were at Ray's mercy to build their future. He would take the lead and open the restaurants himself.

A few years later, Mr. Kroc opened his first restaurant in Des Plaines, Illinois. Built on the premise of fast service, all the mixers were running the first day and never stopped. The more shakes that could be made, the more people that would taste his dream. Ray believed that the essentials of business were in QSC. Quality, Service, and Cleanliness became the doctrine of all his franchises and still exists today. From that first franchise opening in 1955, Ray Kroc and his team changed not only the restaurant business as we know it, but also changed the world of customer service forever.

Milestone after milestone, the McDonald's Corporation expanded into the lives of every American and eventually 100 countries worldwide. The integration of entrepreneurial spirit and customer feedback formed the menu items that we all know today. In 1968, the iconic sandwich named the Big Mac was born by a franchisor named Jim Delligati. Listening to the feedback of his customers in Pittsburgh, he realized they hungered for a larger sandwich than was offered on the existing menu. The flagship burger was born and millions have been made since.

In 1973, another owner operator named Herb Peterson developed a breakfast sandwich named the Egg McMuffin. Never before had Americans viewed breakfast in terms of fast food and service. It was traditionally a sit down at home meal. Shortly after McDonald's put forth their breakfast menu, the American consumer had a new meal to eat out at restaurants. Breakfast menus started popping up everywhere and the competition continues today.

Realizing their impact on children and families, McDonald's gave the ultimate service back to their customers. In 1974, they created the Ronald McDonald house where families of critically ill children could stay while their loved ones were receiving treatments. Since then, the Ronald McDonald House Charities have become a multi-million dollar operation and services children from all over the world.

The Ronald McDonald Care Mobile program brings health services to their customers. These state of the art vehicles deliver low cost medical and dental services directly to needy children in their own neighborhoods. Educational programs are also given in a cost effective manner to families through the mobile facilities.

Today, McDonald's continues to be on the cutting edge of customer service to bring the best to its customers. New concepts have popped up in various areas to serve non-traditional menu items that customers have been demanding. Healthier foods such as baked goods, salads, and fruits are tested in many of the franchises and in such new restaurants like McDonald's Bistro.

In the world of technology, McDonald's has branched out by placing wireless internet in many of their locations. Other services such as ATMs and the acceptance of credit cards are prevalent throughout their franchises. Add to that all of their ventures on the world wide web and McDonald's takes on much more that fast food and fast service.

The service numbers are staggering. In micro terms, McDonald's continues to serve full meals to their guests in a matter of minutes.

Globally, McDonald's is the leading foodservice retailer with more than 30,000 restaurants. They serve more than 52 million people in 100 countries each day. Their icon slogan of "billions served daily" brings light to their scope of service.

Overall, no other food service company has changed the world like McDonald's. When they introduce a new menu item, every other fast food chain follows with their own rendition. Their service with a smile is often attempted but seldom followed through in such a fast paced industry. The undisputable leader in every aspect of customer service, the McDonald's Corporation continually raises the bar for faster, more efficient service in all of their restaurants.

On a final note, I would like to share with you a short experience that occurred in the not so distant past. While pressed for time traveling to one of my seminars, I pulled into a local McDonald's drive thru for a quick bite. Although it was the lunch time rush, the drive thru lane was moving along at an efficient pace and time passed quickly. When I approached the menu board, I was astonished with the McDonald's crew member that greeted me.

Apparently, the speaker communication system had failed at the beginning of the lunch rush. In an effort to maintain high service standards, the restaurant was doing everything they could to take care of the customers. Positioned in the grass next to the ill fated speaker was a crew member with a two-way radio in her hand.

"Welcome to McDonald's," she said with a smile.

"Can I take your order today?"

Every word that was spoken to the crew member was repeated into the radio on its way to the restaurant. Moments later, as I pulled up to the window, my order was completed and handed to me by a member of management.

"Here you go sir. Sorry for the inconvenience. We hope to have the system fixed shortly. Have a great day!"

If service like this was given to millions of people around the globe, how could the world not have a great day?

Who hired THESE people?

17

TIRED OF LOUSY SERVICE???

While driving your van across the state, your sound system goes haywire. The speakers start crackling and you can barely hear the song that is being played. Thinking that it must be the local radio station, you change the dial to a different station. More crackling and interference greet you as you decide to pop in a disc instead. The disc slides into the deck but no music comes out.

After your silent trip is all set and done, you turn your sites to fixing the radio problem. Looking through the yellow pages, you find a local "audio specialist" and decide the time is right. As you pull your van up to the business doors, a sign greets you indicating that the store is "under new ownership". O.K. No problem. You never knew the past owners so no hard feelings. Usually, a change in ownership can be for the better.

The clerk inside the store says that they can replace the system and have the van back to you in two hours. The total bill will be $150. You figure this is a good deal and you leave the van. With no call to indicate a delay, you return in three hours to pick up the van. Now, a different clerk tells you that they ran into a few problems and the job is not done. What kind of problems? He goes into some technical details and the bottom line is that your van won't be ready for a while.

At the end of the day you return to the shop and are greeted by smiling clerks. The van is all set. The two guys present you with a bill for $270. Once your amazement calms down, you talk to the manager who explains that speakers were blown and they had to be replaced. He offers to take the speakers out if you still want to pay the $150, but the system won't play. Sucking up the situation, you pay the man and drive away.

As you drive down the road, an unexplained phenomenon takes over your van. When you put the windows down the lights go off. As you hit the turn signal to turn the van around, your radio volume goes up. Returning to the shop, all the employees have gone home except one clerk. He laughs when you tell him the problem and tells you to return when the manager is in tomorrow.

The following day, you return and the manager assures you that he will correct the problem himself. Hours later your van is returned to you. As you drive away, the electrical system seems to have returned to normal. With a new sense of confidence, you turn on the radio to listen to some tunes. The sound that comes through the speakers is crackling and barely audible. Great, $270 down the drain.

With your tolerance level in the toilet, you call the audio shop to demand service. The manager tells you he's done all the work he can do and any further repairs will cost you more. Seemingly at a dead end, you take the van to another repair shop which costs you $100 more. When you explain the situation to the new mechanic, he advises you to call the Better Business Bureau.

The BBB was set up for just this kind of situation. They record thousands of complaints from consumers like you. Their process entails a full disclosure of your side of the story on an online form. After receiving it, they forward it to the business for a rebuttal. If no response is given, your complaint is recorded as just that, a complaint. If the business responds and the bureau likes their story, the claim is dismissed.

When service fails, do you really care if someone has a judgment about it? You have been dealt a bad hand and you want justice. Just because the company had a good line of bull to react to your complaint, should the whole thing be swept under the rug? Absolutely not. For the justice seekers of the world, there exists a band of super service heroes organized not in the Justice League but at **Angie's List.**

Angieslist.com is a consumer driven service that gives 24 hour access to reports and reviews about service companies across the United States. When you have repairs that need to het done or you have to find a qualified health service professional, all you need to do is contact Angie's List. In all its simplicity, here is how their company works.

The first step to enjoy the benefits of Angie's List is to become a member. For a very small fee, consumers (and consumers only) can become a member and view very detailed reports on every service company imaginable. From electricians to plumbers, handymen to grass cutters, thousands of companies are rated on their service levels by fellow consumers. What a benefit this is! Ask yourself this question. Would you rather see ratings from some magazine or newspaper that stays in business from the ads that these businesses buy; or would you rather have an honest opinion from homeowners just like you that already use their services?

There are currently over 650,000 consumers nationwide that use Angie's List. Every month, those consumers submit more than 15,000 reports about the companies they've hired and the health service providers that they have used. Each one of those reports includes such information as type of service provided, response times, prices, and the quality of work received. They even go as far as to include such information as cleanliness before, during, and after the job and if they were friendly to your family and pets.

Since integrity is crucial in this kind of service reporting, Angie's List goes to great pains to protect the information. As previously stated, entries can be made by consumers only, but companies do have a chance to give a rebuttal. Although no judgment is made right or wrong, both sides of the story are told for all to see. So no company can exercise leverage in the service reports, they are not allowed to advertise or pay to be on the list. In fact, consumers can only report on the same service every six months to ensure that companies do not interfere with the integrity of the list.

Angie's list has become a driving force in the service industry. Their focus on quality has resulted in rave reviews and awards for their website and their magazine. The reports of bad service have resulted in many companies changing the way they do business. If they know a consumer has the ability to give them a review that will be seen by so many other consumers, the quality of their service greatly improves. Consumers hold the power as it should be.

The previous story of the car audio repair shop actually impacted my family. When we turned to the Better Business Bureau, the complaints seemed to fall on deaf ears. The repair shop was given a chance for rebuttal but they did not care enough to reply. They did not reply because they knew that the BBB lost its power of influence in such a large market years ago. If I turned to Angie's List first, perhaps the outcome would have been better. Next time, I'll be armed with their power.

Thank you Angie's List for being a Champion of customer service!

Who hired THESE people?

18

FAMILY DINING AT ITS' BEST!

Every family has their own traditions. Whether they are celebrating a birthday, anniversary, graduation, or some other life event, each family breaks bread in their own fashion. When I was just a young man, all family occasions involved a household of people eating Italian delicacies and filling the house with joy.

As I grew older and created a family of my own, I made it a point to celebrate those same life events in a similar fashion. For years, every holiday meant a feast at the LaPorta house. The more people the merrier. But as the sand in the hour glass pours more rapidly these days, it grows more difficult to hold these elaborate gatherings at our house. The planning and most importantly the cooking, take a great deal of time and effort. Like most families in America today, we have broken away from some family traditions and outsource at least the cooking part. On those all important occasions, we have developed new traditions of going to the same restaurants.

When it's your birthday or the more important anniversary, you want to celebrate with style and finesse. You don't want to worry about all the details and you definitely don't want to worry about the service. You hunger for the comforts of home while not having to deal with the cooking or the cleaning. You want to go where the people are friendly, personable and are there to give you the best quality service available. In the end, you want to go to one of the Darden Restaurants.

In my house, we have six people with all different tastes and appetites. Luckily for us, Darden has a restaurant to suit all tastes. For my oldest daughter, Amber, her birthday always means a trip to Olive Garden. For the teenager, Hope, nothing suits her better than a rib eye from Longhorn Steakhouse. The two youngest kids, Sara and Peter Jr. love to explore the seafood at Red Lobster. Finally, Angel and I change it up depending on the celebration. For our birthdays, I go towards my Italian heritage and go to Olive Garden while she prefers the crab at Red Lobster. For special outings and anniversaries, Darden gives us Bahama Breeze, The Capital Grille, and Seasons 52 to choose from. All in all, there is a restaurant for every occasion.

My choice for Darden Restaurants to be included as a Champion of service stems from all they have done for the American family of today. Much like my own family, every family strives for the ultimate casual dining experience to relax and enjoy. They want their children to be serviced, respected and taken care of. In these trying times, it is just as important that the experience be affordable for the family budget. Darden Restaurants fits all categories.

Upon researching this section on Darden, I contacted their corporate office. It was no surprise to me at all that they were helpful and cooperative to all of my questions. The service that they strive for every day in their restaurants starts at the top and trickles down. When I asked about Darden's core values and purpose, it was not a surprise to find such wholesome values but it was shocking to see how simple their purpose was.

"To nourish and delight everyone we serve"

Plain and simple. No frills or high extravagance have been added to make them sound better. They are a collective group of casual dining restaurants. They are not trying to solve the problems of the world by pretending to be someone they are not. Quite simply, they are producing nourishing food to make sure that every customer is delighted with their meal. Can you imagine if every restaurant in America had the same doctrine? What a wonderful dining world this would be.

In order to drive my vote for the Darden choice to the ballot box, I would like to share an amazing quick story with you. On a recent family outing, we chose to cap off the day with a peaceful dinner at Red Lobster. With so many choices, it was the wise answer to everyone's pallet. We would all get to relax and enjoy dinner while the youngest pair enjoyed their favorites, popcorn shrimp and shrimp alfredo.

Once the family was seated and ready to choose, the server came to our table to take the order. As usual, my wife began by ordering for the two younger ones. To our disappointment, we were informed that they had run out of the sauce they needed to create Sara's shrimp alfredo. Tired and hungry, she began to cry. Understanding the importance of the situation, the server ran off to ask his manager what could be done at this late hour to take care of my daughter.

Returning to the table, the manager and the server informed us that they had a solution to the problem. Across the street was one of their sister restaurants, Olive Garden. The sauce that they used was similar to the one at Olive Garden. The manager made a quick call and the sauce was on its way over to be prepared for young Sara. The trip would cause a slight delay, but all would be taken care of.

In the giant scheme of things, that sauce would not have made or broken the meal. As parents, we would have chosen another selection that Sara probably would have eaten and forgotten about the whole experience. On the flip side of the coin, Sara and her parents were delighted by the simple actions of the server and the manager. They went above and beyond for their customer and won a family's loyalty for life. Thank you, Darden Restaurants, for producing such Champions of Service to serve the great American family.

Who hired THESE people?

19

THE WONDERFUL, MAGICAL, WORLD OF GUEST SERVICE

No discussion, article, or book on guest service is complete without the almighty Walt Disney Company. Spanning the entire globe, this company exemplifies all that is service in whatever avenue they pursue. Movies, media, theme parks and so much more, the message is loud and clear in all of their holdings. They exist to entertain the guest, to take the guest on a journey of magic and imagination, and to take care of every wish the guest may dream of.

It was my honor and privilege to be a leader at Walt Disney World in Florida for many years. Although my viewpoint of this wonderful company is highly skewed, it was the very essence of service that drew me to them in the first place. For many years my wife and kids had made the trek to Orlando a few times a year. From the very first time I set foot on their property, I knew that I had to be a part of it. Since that first day so many years ago, no matter where I go on this planet, I compare all service received to Disney. They are the mold, the model, and the inspiration of service all rolled into one.

Regardless of your walk of life, Disney's long reach has touched you in some way. Perhaps it was in your youth, while you sat with your parents on a Sunday night and watched *The Wonderful World of Disney* on television. Perhaps it has been a favorite movie, print ad, or a favorite character. Families from around the globe flock to their numerous theme parks or take a cruise on one of their ships, just to return home with unforgettable memories of extraordinary service.

To attempt a complete listing of their services in all of Disney's endeavors would be an injustice to this remarkable company. Every experience is different, but their ideology is the same in every corner of the world. Let's start, however, at the very beginning. The starting line for every employee (or cast member as they are called) in the Walt Disney Company, is the Casting Building.

When a perspective applicant is interested in working at Disney, they can take one of two routes. The ever popular online application is taken only after a series of introductory messages are forwarded to the applicant. Once the web page is opened, the music fills your senses as images of smiling, happy cast members are paraded before you. In their various elements, all of these pictured employees have one thing in common. They are all serving guests in some way. Children, parents, young and old, all of the guests pictured are being taken care of enthusiastically by the most magical people in the world. The application and information follows later, once the seeker has been pulled into this wonderful world of service.

The same holds true for your trip to the casting building. I cannot tell you of the experiences in any of their other casting offices, but I can take you on a short journey into the Walt Disney World hiring offices in Florida.

The journey begins, of course, as you travel through their extensive property in Lake Buena Vista, Florida. As you arrive, you pass so many messages of magic and wonder that your senses are in overdrive before you get out of the car. Characters dancing on signs, animated billboards, and listings for resorts, theme parks, and water parks invite all that travel to this amazing world. As the applicant arrives at the casting center they are greeted by golden characters adorning the outside and lobby of this building. Before they encounter the first cast member, they climb a ramp to the second floor that subliminally tells the applicant they are rising to a new level of company. The walls along the ramp are covered with paintings of characters and Walt Disney himself. Overall, you are submerged into their brand, their essence, their message.

As you await the interview process, each applicant is treated to a video of the company. In every scene, service and fun are the messages. Guests and cast members interacting in shops, in restaurants, and on attractions. Resort videos are shown with exuberant guests getting world class service in all that the resorts offer. Pool service and room service are all part of the preview as cast members go above and beyond in resort operations. When all of your senses are filled with magic and wonder, you are ready for the interview and hiring process.

The whole meaning for this short journey has been to show you that guest service for the Walt Disney Company is not something they practice or strive for. It is everything to them. All studies on their worldwide popularity and continued growth all come down to the fact that they breathe, eat, and sleep guest service. There is nothing more crucial to their operations and no one more important than the guest.

Once hired, new cast members go through an intensive training process stressing service every step of the way. They use terms like "honor" and "tradition" simultaneously while discussing their world class service. Regardless of their previous experience, every cast member becomes service experts and continually challenged to find new ways to serve their guests. The recognition programs that identify and reward excellent service in the Disney Company are so extensive it would take another book to explain them all. In the end, every cast member becomes ambassadors of service.

Every cast member in the Walt Disney Company could tell you endless stories of amazing service. They are not once in a lifetime occurrences, but magical moments that wow the guests every day. All the departments, from housekeeping to the front desk, from ride attractions to food and beverage, have service tales abound. What they take for granted as their basic steps forward, would put any other service company to shame.

In resort operations, the Disney team takes a normal overnight stay and raises the bar through the stratosphere. If it is your birthday or anniversary, you may find a complimentary basket in your room or an autographed picture of your favorite character. If an illness or some other event has dampened your vacation experience, that very same character may be knocking on your door to brighten up your day. Before they can even dream of asking for one, a cast member presents balloons and stickers for the young ones. In each room, on every bed, the housekeepers keep you entertained as your linen is transformed into various animals. Special requests are not shunned upon but welcomed as a challenge by the extraordinary guest service departments.

From a theme park perspective, each department strives to be the best service providers. The park service people are quick to offer a change of clothes if your loved ones become sick on a ride. The attractions folks are quick to replace that stuffed animal your child lost on the last ride. Not happy with your meal, the food and beverage will do whatever it takes to make you happy before you leave. No request is too much, no service is too small. For every need, there is a service. For every service, an enthusiastic cast member is there providing it.

Since my enthusiasm for this wonderful company knows no boundaries, I will wrap up this discussion with a tale of my own. While I wore many different leadership hats at Disney, one of my favorites was my time as a leader for the Coronado Springs Convention Resort on their Florida property. During that time, I was privy to hundreds of outstanding deeds from my team to our cherished guests. The convention business gave a whole new world of opportunities to serve and we explored every one of them.

One such opportunity presented itself inside the merchandise shop. In addition to general merchandise sales for a resort, this shop provided many services to our guests. One such service was a photo processing service that allowed the guests a chance to drop off their film after their day in the parks and the pictures would be ready for them the next day. Before the guest could go home, their memories were captured on film and ready to show off to whomever they encountered. An excellent service to provide while on vacation.

On this particular occasion, there was a convention in house for an advertising firm. As part of their convention happenings, the ad execs were hosting a competition to see which one of their star players could come up with the best ad pitch for a given campaign. As luck would have it, one of the ad teams lost part of their presentation traveling to the convention. Their only salvation was that they had taken photographs of the missing items and the images were stored in their digital camera.

In between sessions, the two person ad team rushed into the merchandise shop. The cast member that greeted them was Paul. As their story unfolded, Paul listened carefully to their instructions. They needed the pictures back in two hours, immediately following a mandatory meeting. Although the photo service that Disney offered was next day developing, Paul told the pair he would do his best.

After the pitch men left the store, Paul phoned the photo service location to see if they could assist. Unfortunately, even at the best rerouting available, the pictures would not be back for many hours. Taking service to the next level, Paul decided to do whatever necessary to service his guests.

On his lunch break, Paul took his personal vehicle and drove off property with the digital file. Finding the closest Walgreens Drug Store, he explained the predicament and the pictures were ready in minutes. He returned to the resort a short time later with the pictures in hand.

When the ad men arrived, they had a look of defeat on their face. They knew that there was slim to no chance that they would get their pictures. They would fail their ad pitch for sure. Luck was with them that day because it was a Disney cast member they asked for service, and it was outstanding service that they received. The photo images were perfect and just in time for their presentation. Later that day, they returned with a world of thanks as victory was theirs. The ad pitch was perfect, especially with the photographs. Upon their exit, they exclaimed that anywhere else in the world they would have failed, if not for the great service of Disney.

Thank you Walt Disney Company for being champions of guest service!

Who hired THESE people?

20

CONCLUSION

"Service is eternal"

An odd closing quote, it exemplifies the basic premise of this book. Customer service should never end for a business or organization. It is not just a catchy phrase or something that we do in addition to our other duties during the day. Customer service should be the sole purpose to be in business. If it is not, it is a guarantee that the business will fail. Service should never stop until the business is no longer a business.

At this point, I could rehash many of the lessons that were presented to you in this book. Besides being repetitive, I do not want to cloud your memory of some of the stories that you read. Instead I want to instill a final thought about responsibility.

Responsibility is a two sided coin with the consumer and the business on opposite sides. On one side, the consumer is responsible for seeking out, requesting, and obtaining the products and services that they desire. A business cannot make those decisions for you and should not try to. You, the consumer, should take the responsibility to obtain great service and not be distracted or settle for anything less.

On the business side, it is your sole responsibility to make sure that your organization provides the best service possible to all customers, without prejudice or hesitation. For every customer that walks through your doors, calls your phone, or pulls up your web site, your responsibility increases. For mega businesses such as Wal-Mart, your responsibility lies not only to the individual but to the country collectively. If you can draw in such astronomical amounts of revenue that you actually change the nation's Gross National Product, you can take the time to train everyone of your team to provide the best quality service.

If each one of the leaders of industry would simply take the responsibility to make customer service their sole priority, the world would change overnight. As consumers, it is time to take a stand and demand nothing less than the best service. The future depends on us. If we continue to accept poor service and self service as the norm, there will be no service left for our children. I think they are worth the effort.

AUTHOR NOTE

The best part about second chances is the opportunity to change tomorrow's sunrise. The sun will still come up on the same part of the world, but you can make a difference to the people that wake up to it. I can truly call this book a success if it changed you in some way or touched your life.

The book itself has had more than the average share of second chances. The writing began almost immediately after the last book was completed. Unfortunately, my earnest to complete the book at breakneck speeds got the best of me. I failed to create hard copies in either digital or paper forms. When my computer crashed from an awful virus, all the work was destroyed with nothing to show for it.

The second time around, I proceeded with much more caution. I saved each and every word onto a disc that I carried with me everywhere. One evening at home, I made the mistake of leaving the disc on my desk while I made dinner with my wife. When I returned to my desk, I was met with writer terror as I viewed my son breaking the disc into pieces. The second draft was dead.

The third and final draft was saved in every way known to man. I wanted to make sure that the world actually got to read this copy and apparently I succeeded. The finished product is much different than the original version and I hope you enjoyed reading it.

At this time, I'd like to thank my family for their passion and understanding. I continue to juggle many things in my professional life and they continue to stand by me day after day. I'd also like to thank all the bad service providers without which I would not have a book on service to write about.

My life has been filled with passion. As a Capricorn, I am told that passion is my destiny. My first passion was music. Performing music and listening to it has always motivated me to achieve new heights. The second passion in my life has been my wife and children. They have taken over my world since the first moment I met my wife.

The two great passions in my career life have been leadership and customer service. Every business I encounter is judged within these two realms. Now that I have completed a book on each of them, the subject matter for future books will unveil itself with future sunrises. The circle is complete.

Thank you for spending this time with me, constant reader, for time is life and life is short. "Live as though today is your last, and work as if you will live forever".

Kissimmee, Florida, 2008

About The Author

Peter A. LaPorta is the President and Founder of LaPorta Enterprises. His first book, "Ignite the Passion, A Guide to Motivational Leadership", was published and released worldwide in 2003 by 1ˢᵗ Books Library, later named Author House.

Throughout his sparkling career, Peter has touched thousand of lives through his leadership and dedication to customer service. Raised in the small town of Monroe, Connecticut, and attending the University of Connecticut, Peter built upon a solid base of New England family ethics.

Currently based in Central Florida, Peter and his wife, Angel, raise four children, Amber, Hope, Sara, and Peter Jr., while operating LaPorta Enterprises as a global consulting firm. Peter's seminars and keynote speaker addresses carry him around the world and back, spreading his motivational words to many, both here and abroad.

A former Disney leader, Peter's career spans three decades with twenty four years in the leadership arena. Small businesses to corporate giants, Peter's attention to ethics and integrity in the daily work place is unparalleled. The motivation of his employees and satisfaction of his countless customers are a testimonial of his career accomplishments in the often chaotic business world.

Every day, Peter carries the torch to "Ignite the Passion" of every person he comes into contact with. Student, employee, customer or client, he seeks to learn from all and touch each life along the way. For more information on Peter's remarkable journey and accomplishments, visit ***http://laportaenterprises.com***.

LaPorta Enterprises

Since 1990, LaPorta Enterprises has worked with thousands of people around the globe, bringing home the messages for a smoother work force through individual motivation.

We offer you…

- Keynote Speakers and presentations
- Seminar and Conference presentations
- Individualized subject matter
- Customized breakout workshops
- Full consulting services
- Signed copies of Peter's books.
- Full line of retail products
- Much, much, more…

All presentations are sculptured to you, our client, your people, and your organization.

For more information, contact our website at
http://laportaenterprises.com

or email us at
office.manager@laportaenterprises.com